WITHDRAWN

My Organic Life

ALFRED A. KNOPF
1915 · 100 YEARS · 2015

NORA POUILLON

My Organic Life

How a Pioneering Chef
Helped Shape
the Way We Eat Today

WITH LAURA FRASER

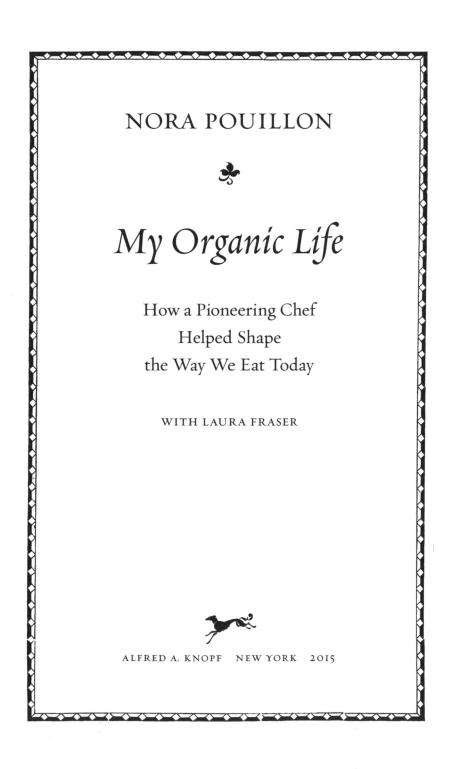

ALFRED A. KNOPF   NEW YORK   2015

THIS IS A BORZOI BOOK
PUBLISHED BY ALFRED A. KNOPF

Published in the United States by Alfred A. Knopf,
a division of Penguin Random House LLC, New York,
and distributed in Canada by Random House of Canada,
a division of Penguin Random House Ltd., Toronto.

www.aaknopf.com

Knopf, Borzoi Books, and the colophon are registered
trademarks of Penguin Random House LLC.

Library of Congress Cataloging-in-Publication Data
Pouillon, Nora, author.
My organic life : how a pioneering chef helped shape the way we eat today /
Nora Pouillon.—First edition.
pages cm
ISBN 978-0-385-35075-4 (hardcover)—ISBN 978-0-385-35076-1 (eBook)
1. Pouillon, Nora. 2. Women cooks—United States—Biography.
3. Cooks—United States—Biography. 4. Cooking (Natural foods)
5. Organic living. I. Title.
TX649.P65A3 2015
641.5092—dc23
[B]   2014036931

Jacket photograph © 1974 by Margaret Thomas/The Washington Post
Jacket design by Abby Weintraub and Carol Devine Carson

Photograph page 166 © by Daniel Mahdavian Photography.
Photograph page 220 © by The Washington Post. Photograph page 246
© by Adam Barnes. All other photographs courtesy of the author.

Manufactured in the United States of America
First Edition

This book is dedicated to my parents,
sisters, and all of my children;
and of course, my business partners and
all my friends, who have supported me
throughout my organic journey.

This book is also written for all the chefs
who have endured me and whom I may have
inspired, as well as my staff in the kitchen and
dining room, who have been so loyal.

Contents

My Organic Life

❧

Amuse Bouche

Over the past thirty years at Restaurant Nora, as I've made the rounds in the dining room, countless people have asked me, "Why do you care so much about organic food?" They want to know why I am so passionate about this subject that I was driven to create the world's first entirely organic restaurant, where everything—from the produce and meat to the oil, salt, and coffee—is certified organic.

The quick answer is simply health: organic food is better for our bodies and our environment.

The longer answer begins with a side of beef.

In the early 1970s, not long after I had moved to Washington, D.C., from my native Austria with my French husband, Pierre, we began entertaining a lot. We didn't have much money to go out to restaurants, so I started giving dinner parties. These turned into catering jobs and then small cooking classes in my home.

It wasn't long before I realized that I needed to buy meat wholesale rather than retail in order to make my catering and classes profitable. So I looked up "beef" in the Yellow Pages and found some ads for sides of beef, which could be stored for me in a freezer locker. This was all new to me: I pictured a side of beef hanging, whole, in a locker, with my name written on it, and wondered how I'd even begin to butcher it.

I called up one place on the Eastern Shore and asked about its meat.

"It's Angus beef," the woman who answered the phone told me. "Wonderfully marbled."

She knew the secret, she said proudly, to turning out the most succulent meat I'd ever tasted: she fed her cattle corn for the last two months of their lives so they'd be fat and tender. "It's prime Angus beef, honey," she said. "It melts in your mouth like butter."

I was taken aback. Where I grew up, cows ate grass. Corn was for chickens. That seemed like a fundamental rule of nature.

"Corn?" I asked. "Cows don't eat corn."

Normally, no, she agreed, cows don't eat corn, because they can't digest it. So she fed them antibiotics to help them digest the corn without getting sick. The antibiotics—laced into the feed—also prevented illnesses that came from the "feedlot lifestyle." She also told me she administered growth-promoting hormones through a funnel inserted behind the animals' ears so they would eat more and get fatter faster.

I felt ill. All this time, I had been feeding my husband, two young children, and friends meats that were marbled not only with extra fat—who needs extra fat?—but with hormones and antibiotics. I felt as if every steak I'd thrown on the grill had been slowly poisoning them. As I hung up, I was ready to swear off meat forever.

Then I noticed another ad in the Yellow Pages: "I Sell Natural Beef." Who knew? At this point, it seemed worth a shot. The man who answered, a Mr. Koenig, was a farmer from Pennsylvania. When I asked about his beef, instead of telling me all the things he did to his cows, he told me all the things he didn't do. He did not give his animals antibiotics. No growth-promoting hormones. No corn feed, only grass or hay. No confining pens, no fumigating the carcasses. (Imagine: fumigating the carcasses!)

He told me how he treated his cows. "I'm very careful not to stress my animals when I take them to slaughter," he said. This was not only for humane reasons, he explained. "If an animal is frightened, the adrenal glands overproduce fight-or-flight hormones, which affect the taste and texture of the meat in a bad way," he said. "Basically, you're eating stressed-out muscle."

I told Mr. Koenig I wanted to buy some of his natural beef, but the transaction would prove much more complicated than I had expected. "I'll call you back with directions for where to meet me," he said. The next morning, he called with instructions to meet at a spot in Chevy Chase, Maryland. "Three o'clock sharp," he said. "Wait for me."

The following day, I set out with my young sons, Alexis

and Olivier, in the backseat of the car. When we arrived, there was no mistaking the pickup spot: five station wagons were already waiting. When Mr. Koenig arrived in a lumbering white van, the women in the cars opened their doors simultaneously and ran to circle the van's back door. Mr. Koenig, ropy and small with wire-rimmed glasses, began calling out last names as he doled out cooler boxes and stuffed checks into his jacket pocket. He kept glancing around anxiously, as if he were selling coolers full of fake watches or marijuana. It was all over in a moment, and he tore off in his van.

"You're new," observed the woman parked next to me as she closed her trunk. I nodded. When I remarked that it had all seemed like a drug deal, she laughed and explained that while it wasn't the same thing, it was in fact illegal to transport across state lines meat that hadn't been slaughtered in a federally inspected facility, especially in an unrefrigerated vehicle. It hardly mattered to her. "I have to eat clean food," she said. She had just finished treatment for cancer a few months before. Several of the people waiting for the meat, she told me, were recovering from serious illnesses. She was convinced that the chemicals lacing her food were at least partly responsible for making her sick. And it wasn't just beef, she told me. Antibiotics and hormones were also pumped into our chicken and pork. "Pesticides and fungicides are on our fruits and vegetables, and chemical fertilizers are in everything. We're poisoning every cell in our bodies."

As I drove home with my children, I felt certain that I was right to seek out alternatives to what was commercially available at the time. I felt strongly that animals should be able to wander freely and eat grass, as I remembered from my childhood in the Austrian countryside. My suspicions about the food we ate every day—the squishy white bread with no nutritional value, the mayonnaise-laden sandwiches, the packaged snacks, the TV dinners, the canned-soup casseroles—seemed justified. These foods were too far from nature, too processed, too removed from the fresh, just-picked produce I'd grown up with.

And so I decided I wasn't just going to teach my students how to cook. I was going to teach them how to cook healthfully, to make natural, wholesome food that also tasted delicious. From that moment on, as much as I could, I was going to seek out food free from pesticides, hormones, antibiotics, and other chemical additives. I wanted my family and friends to be healthy. I had a new mission, and though I couldn't fully articulate it at the time, it was to lead an organic life and to help others to do the same.

CHAPTER I

Tyrol

I am a war child. Although the war ended when I was just eighteen months old, I am surprised by how much I remember. Maybe it is because the events were so traumatic; maybe it is because the deprivations of the war years blended into those of the postwar years. My earliest memory is of a terrifying sound: a high-pitched siren blaring through our house in Vienna. My mother would grab my older sisters, pick me up, and rush us all down to the cellar. There, we would sit on benches or on the dirt floor, huddled with our neighbors, awaiting the explosions. Shivering and closing my eyes tight, I would try to tune out the noise. I would breathe in the damp, earthy smell of the cellar, where my mother stored fresh apples, pears, potatoes, and glass jars filled with eggs from our chickens to last through the winter. Those rich smells transported me to a quieter place—the warm, sunny farm in the mountains where the fruits and vegetables grew—and comforted me until the raid was over.

The war disrupted everything, and because I was very young, disruption was all I knew of life. My memories, like Vienna at the time, are shadowy. I know, partly through the stories my family members have told me, that people on the streets were hungry, some were disappearing, and there was a hushed sense of desperation. Everywhere, food was scarce. Farmers had gone to war and left their fields fallow. Food was not something that you could take for granted but rather something that had to be rationed, saved, bartered, or traded on the black market. In Vienna, food seemed very distant from the country fields where it was grown.

But I was lucky to be able to spend most of the war outside the city, in the place I dreamed about during those air raids: a farm in the Tyrolean mountains. Even before I was born—in 1943—my father had decided that he needed to send his family away from Vienna while the war raged. He was a successful businessman and able to lease a working farm a day's distance away so that my mother, my two older sisters, and I would have a safe place to weather the devastation and its aftermath—and have plenty of fresh food to eat. My father was an outdoorsman who loved hiking and healthy eating, so a remote farmhouse in the Alps seemed like the best place for him to send us.

Later, I came to understand there was another reason he had sequestered us in such a remote place: we were also hiding Jewish friends from the Nazis. But I knew nothing of that then. For the duration of the war, with the exception of occasional trips to Vienna, we were tucked away high in the mountains of Tyrol.

I lived in the mountains, off and on, from just after I was born until I was eight years old. The farm my sisters and I grew up on was one of those magical places of childhood, not only because it was safe and comforting—the opposite of war-torn Vienna—but also because it was the place where I awoke to the world with a sense of wonder. More than anything else in my first decade of life, the experience of living on a working farm profoundly influenced the person I was to become. There, in fields on steep mountain slopes, with a chalet-style log house, I discovered how food is grown and how it tastes just pulled from the soil or warmed by the sun. Far from the rubble of Vienna, the food in Tyrol gave me my first taste of nature's bounty—something that has stayed with me all my life.

Mutti, my mother, always loved to tell the story of how I was born, and she repeated it every year on my birthday. The farmhouse in Tyrol was a two-hour hike down steep mountain trails to the nearest village, Kirchberg. Right before I was born, Mutti hid pork, bread, and other food from the farm in her suitcase and the lining of her coat—you were not allowed to carry food back and forth to Vienna—and thus encumbered, nine months pregnant, clambered down the mountain to the village. She was headed for Vienna so that she could give birth in the same hospital where my sisters were born and be closer to my father. From Kirchberg, she caught a train to Vienna, which lasted six or seven hours, or perhaps even longer, because of all the military inspections. The train was frequently halted so that the officers could check everyone's papers; when the Germans annexed Austria in 1938, my parents had to produce documentation going back three generations in order to prove they had no Jewish blood. My mother's papers were in order, but she still held her breath to see if she would be searched and caught smuggling food. Anything could happen to you in those days for the slightest infraction; everyone lived in fear. Eventually, she made it to the hospital, which was marked on the roof with a big X to make it clear it should not be bombed. Amid the explosions going off all around in Vienna, I was born, and a couple of weeks later my mother made the long trip back to Tyrol with her new infant.

Later, on occasional trips to and from Vienna, I would learn for myself what an adventure it was to reach the farm. I recall leaving Vienna at dawn in my father's car, driven by "Herr Krakover" the chauffeur, and driving for hours along winding icy roads. Today the journey would take five hours, but then it took all day. The trip was long, boring, and probably dangerous, but all I can remember is what I ate. Throughout the long journey, my sisters and I savored the Wiener schnitzel sandwiches that Mutti had prepared on dark bread, making them last as many miles as possible. Sometimes we would stop at a butchers for our favorite *Leberkäsesemmel,* which is a kind of roasted-liver pâté. You slice it like cheese, but it's more like a mortadella. You serve it hot, in thick slices. It's baked so it has a crunchy crust, and you eat it with mustard and pickles on a kaiser roll. This was a real highlight for us.

Finally, when it was night, we would arrive in Kirchberg, where my parents had friends who owned a grocery store and where we could sleep overnight. You couldn't just pull up to an inn at the time; there were very few places to stay, and people were cautious and fearful, wary of strangers who might denounce them to the Germans. Only old acquaintances would risk taking you in. We were tired, cold, and hungry by then, so it was wonderful when the owner's wife would give us thin slices of *Kletzenbrot*—a dark sourdough bread filled with dried apples, pears, and hazelnuts—which we spread with her homemade butter. Several slices of *Kletzenbrot*, with a glass of fresh milk, were our dinner. At that point in time, you couldn't find *Kletzenbrot* in Vienna; it was truly a regional specialty. They used what they had on hand to make it—rye flour, along with the fruits and nuts—and incorporated it into their daily sourdough bread and made something special out of it. To us, it tasted delicious—an almost fancy snack that gave us a feeling of comfort and safety at a time when traveling was precarious.

At night, we all climbed into one bed—a rough linen bag filled with straw—and covered ourselves with an eiderdown duvet, snuggling close to keep warm on a night so cold that in the morning a skin of ice had formed on the windowpanes.

At first light, we pulled on our long underwear, wool trousers, anoraks, and hiking boots for the rest of the journey, which was several miles by foot. We walked up a trail next to a creek, a torrent rushing down from the snowfields on the high peaks. I loved to dawdle, breaking the delicate ice at the edges of the stream with my toe and watching it crackle into patterns, but Mutti pulled me along. On the way, the pine trees in the snow looked like thousands of Christmas trees, ice crystals sparkling in the sunlight.

It was a long hike to the farmhouse, but my entire family loved being in the outdoors. After hours of trudging up the valley, we finally spotted the A-frame log house, a simple chalet perched on a piece of land hacked out of the hillside. There was one last, impossibly steep hill to climb, but anticipating being inside gave me the energy for the final push. The farmer's wife, Nanni, and their daughter, Moidi, came out to greet us. They ushered us into their warm kitchen, which was heated by a large iron cookstove. The room's warmth enveloped me: I felt cozy, safe, and protected.

We were fortunate to be so well cared for in the farmhouse, far from the war. My sisters and I were too young to understand about Nazis and what was happening in Vienna and around the world. We only vaguely understood that when we heard planes overhead, we had to run inside and cover our ears, waiting for the big explosion. Whatever bombs weren't used on Vienna were dumped in the countryside, and we would come across enormous holes in the fields around the farm. No one ever said it out loud, but everyone secretly feared that one day we too would be hit.

We were also far too young to realize that the friends who came to live with us on the farm, Tante Hertha and her daughter, Herthi, were in danger. As I grew older, I thought we brought them along because Herthi was my friend and I liked to play with her. But it was not until I was a grown woman, living on my own in the United States, that I learned that Tante Hertha, the wife of one of my father's good friends, was Jewish, and in actuality we were protecting them. I still don't know how they managed their journey to the farm, and I certainly doubt that the farmer and his wife knew we were sheltering Jews; no one asked questions at the time or wanted to know. Now I think that hiding our friends was one of the main reasons my father leased such a remote house, unreachable except by a two-hour hike, perched like a lookout at the top of the valley. No one would have taken the time to search the farm without good reason, and we would have seen soldiers coming long before they arrived, with time to hide our friends. If my mother was concerned, she didn't show it, and I remained blissfully unaware of the danger. I think that this was a reason my mother didn't want us to socialize too much with others in the area; she didn't want them to know what we were up to. Happily, Herthi and I are friends to this day, and Tante Hertha and my mother were the same way. I can't bring myself to think of what might have happened to her if she had not been with us on the farm during those years.

By today's standards, the farmhouse was primitive: there was no electricity and no running water. But for a child, it was paradise. We could run freely in the land around the house—so unlike Vienna just after the war, where soldiers patrolled bombed-out streets—and the workings of the subsistence farm were an endless source of fascination for me. I loved to watch Nanni and Alois, her husband, milking cows, cutting wheat and grass, planting and picking vegetables, baking bread, butchering animals, and building and fixing what they needed. They did almost everything themselves, producing all their food, soap, shingles for the roof, yarn, firewood—everything but the iron tools they bought in the village. I was a curious child and soon started poking my nose everywhere on the farm to find out how things worked.

Over the years in the mountains, I gradually felt as if I became a part of the farm and of its way of life. I became more and more aware of the workings of the world around me. I learned that food comes from nature—from the air and the water, the soil and the sun—and that nature must be carefully tended and respected. I saw how much planning and hard work it took to keep a family alive through the whole year and how dreadful it was to waste any of the fruits of those labors. For Nanni and Alois, her husband, food was a constant occupation, and the land was precious. Food was life.

The farm worked according to the rhythms of the day and of the seasons. Every morning and evening, Nanni would milk the two cows. She poured the milk she collected into a separator and turned the handle, and out of one tube came milk and out of the other, cream. Cream was like gold to them. After the war in Vienna, we got used to eating dollops of whipped cream on our desserts, but here that was an unheard-of extravagance. Nanni would collect the cream until she had enough to make butter—a task she performed every two weeks. I would watch as she poured the cream into a big wooden barrel with a handle and began to churn it. When the cream became clumpy, she would add ice-cold water from the spring to rinse off the butterfat. She shaped the butter into loaves with her hands, then rolled them with a wooden tool that imprinted a design on top. Every farm had its own design so you could always know where the butter came from. I loved that detail—that added touch that showed a pride in their work, a way of caring for the food and its provenance and for the simple beauty of what you ate.

Our families ate separately, but the smells of their kitchen during mealtime always drew me to the door. They had their big meal in the middle of the day, after a morning of chores and before an afternoon of even more hard work; it was the only time during the day that they sat down. Nanni would catch me peeking behind the door. "Nora!" she would call, with a smile, "Come in, come in. Come and eat with us." She would make space for me on the wooden bench where they sat, her long gray braid swinging under her scarf, her clogs clumping on the wooden floor.

I knew Mutti would be furious if she found out I accepted their invitation to lunch, because she thought I was intruding and shouldn't eat their food. Now I also see that she worried, perhaps, that I might say something that would give Herthi and her family away. But instead she would scold me. "Their family needs some time to themselves!" she would say in a sharp voice. But I couldn't resist. On one side of the kitchen wall stood a wood-burning stove that was regularly stoked. On top of the stove, corn mush—like polenta—was bubbling in a wide, blackened copper pan. Nanni, a woman with legs like sticks under her full dirndl skirt, would stir and stir the mush with her lean, sinewy arms. When it was finished, she put the whole pan on a wooden trivet on the whitewashed table, which was covered with a homespun tablecloth. Nanni made a big indentation with the back of the spoon in the middle of the corn mush and placed an enormous pad of butter in it, which slowly melted.

With spoons in hand, we began to eat the polenta from our sides of the pan and worked our way toward the middle, where the golden butter pooled. It was like a game, seeing who would get to the treasure first. This was my favorite part. In between bites, we would spoon milk out of a bowl to drink. Sometimes there was a little *Speck* to go with the corn mush or some green beans or other vegetables. But mostly I remember that simple, comforting taste of warm corn and butter. I have always loved to eat simple, good food.

After lunch, we would lick our spoons, wipe them on the tablecloth, and put them back in the drawer, which was under the table—dishes done! There weren't endless plates, glasses, and silver to clean up, as there were when my family ate. We often ate vegetable and bean stews or chicken soup with dumplings, along with bread and butter and sometimes *Speck,* if there was some to be had. Outside, Moidi and I would put some small pebbles and sand in the cooking skillet to clean it, finally rinsing it in the big trough where the water from the spring collected.

Once a week, Nanni made bread, which took her nearly all day. The flour from the bread came from the wheat and rye grown on the farm, which they would cut with big scythes. I remember watching the men cutting the stalks, and the whistling sound it would make, stopping every so often to take a whetstone out of a pocket on their belt to sharpen the blade before beginning again. Later, they threshed the grain and milled it by hand to turn it into flour.

Nanni would take some of her sourdough starter, work in some warm water and more flour with a pinch of sugar, and let it stand until it rose. She'd pull off some of the starter to save for the following week, then begin adding flour. Over the course of the day, she would knead the dough, add more flour and spices (mostly caraway seeds and salt), let it rest, and then knead it again. All that kneading developed more flavor and made it lighter. In between, she worked in the fields, and in the evenings she would do her other chores—spinning the lamb's wool into yarn, knitting the yarn into the wool socks and caps her family wore, or cleaning the kerosene lamps.

Eventually, she would form the dough into seven big round loaves—one for each day of the week. She would bake the bread, at a fairly low temperature, for nearly two hours. On the day she baked, the house smelled like heaven; it was the one day I didn't want to go outside, because I wanted to be wrapped in that warm, rich, earthy smell. When the bread had finished baking, she would bless it—three crosses on the backside of each loaf, one for the Father, the Son, and the Holy Ghost—and say a few words of prayer. This, too, impressed me deeply, the giving thanks for our food, the source of life.

In later years, I would try to make bread as Nanni did. But

for all my experience as a chef, it never turned out half as well as hers. Mine would taste good, but compared with Nanni's, it lacked texture and always emerged as heavy as a doorstop.

The farm wasted nothing. Because there was no running water, we had to carry buckets from the water trough, where there was a spigot that ran down a pipe from the spring uphill. The water was so cold, full of minerals, and delicious; it never tasted better than cupped between my hands right from the source. To bathe, we hauled bucket after bucket into the house, which Mutti heated on the kitchen stove. Then we carried the buckets into our living room, which was heated by a tiled ceramic oven, the *Kachelofen,* so the room was nice and toasty on bath day. Mutti put the tin bathtub in front of the *Kachelofen,* and because I was the youngest and smallest, I got to bathe first. Then came Rosi, my older sister, and then Christa, the oldest. By the end of all the baths, the water was so dirty we would use it to wash our socks. Then we would take the bathwater out of the tub in buckets and pour it on the plants outside.

The farm even made use of our human waste. The farmhouse had a balcony wrapped around it, and at the end of the balcony was a little hut, which was the outhouse. I was scared to go to the outhouse, especially at night, because we only had small kerosene lights, which were not bright enough to frighten away the spiders and God knows what else lurked in there. I would beg one of my sisters to come with me. Inside, there was a wooden seat with a hole, and underneath, two flights down, was the compost pile. Everything went straight onto that pile, including the tidy squares of newspaper we used as toilet paper. The farmer would take all the manure and straw from the barn and add it to the pile, which was the perfect mix for compost. Years later, in my own garden, I would struggle to find the right recipe for the compost—it's tough to get the correct proportions of ingredients so it combusts, not rots—but he had the perfect mix. Today, at the restaurant, we collect vegetable trimmings, eggshells, coffee grinds, oyster shells—layered with straw—and then the compost starts its cooking. Anything but animal matter, and it needs to be turned on a regular basis. After several months, the compost ended up as dark, even, loamy soil, which smelled clean and sweet and nourished the garden. The farmer even collected the liquid compost from the pile, which was sprayed on the fields.

Composting is the most important aspect of organic farming; it's all about the fertility of the soil, which is teaming with life and microorganisms. To preserve the soil is therefore fundamental, as it is an essential source of energy and life for us.

The animals—cows and chickens, a few sheep, and pigs—roamed the hills, digging in the soil, eating grass. They ate food from the same soil we did. We knew better than to give them names, because they would end up on our plates, eventually, as *Speck,* bacon, lamb stew, or chicken legs. The farm family used every part of any animal they butchered—something I still do at Restaurant Nora.

I used to watch my grandmother Omi kill the chickens. Most people just chopped off their heads, and the birds would go flapping around, spurting blood. But my grandmother had a wonderful system. She took a chicken and held it under her arm, wedged between her body and her elbow. Then she held its head and quickly slit its throat with a sharp knife. When it stopped moving, she took its feet, bound them, and hung the chicken upside down to bleed out over a bucket. She would put a piece of newspaper around the cut at the throat and tie it to make it look tidy, not gaping wide. Then she plucked the chicken, which you have to do while it is still warm. She kept the tail feathers, tied them together, and used them as pastry brushes.

It was unbelievable what came out of the bird. Omi carefully took out the entrails—if you accidentally squish the bile, it spoils the whole liver—and then she showed me all the unformed eggs a chicken has inside it. The chicken gizzard was beautiful. She would cut around it and unfold it, and you could see what the chicken ate, including many little stones, which Omi said they needed to digest their food, grinding up the worms and corn. Then she'd cut off the head and legs, pop out the eyes, put water on to boil, scald the head and feet, and with a knife scrape them clean. She would cut out the tongue and the comb for a special omelet, and then the chicken was ready for roasting. She would use the feet, gizzards, and neck for chicken stock.

After the animals were butchered, Alois would boil all the bones with some lye to make soap in a big cauldron outdoors. Unlike bread day, I hated soap day, because it smelled awful. But eventually the smell stopped, and the goop was poured into wooden molds to cool, hardening into decorated rectangles of brown soap. They were beautiful, like Savon de Marseille. I wondered that something that started out smelling so bad could end up smelling delicious—and make you nice and clean.

The vegetable garden was near the house, on a fairly flat patch of ground near the *Eschenbaum*, or ash tree, and surrounded by smaller hazelnut bushes and flowering fruit trees. After the long, cold winter months, early spring brought blossoms everywhere, falling from the trees like snow. Vegetables began to poke up in the garden, and a lush carpet of green spread up the flanks of the mountains to the snowcapped peaks.

First to arrive in spring were the strawberries, which I picked like little gems. They grew nestled in straw and were warm from the sun. They had so much flavor, picked right there, bursting with sweetness. Later the fruit trees flowered and became heavy with sour cherries, apples, and pears. We kids would climb the trees to pick the cherries, which Nanni preserved for the next winter. My favorite of the fruits were the cherries, which were so juicy that they dripped all over our clothing, leaving stains that never came out in the laundry. Because of that, my sisters and I always ate cherries naked. On a warm day, we would strip off our shirts and bite into the warm cherries, letting the juice dribble where it would.

Inside the wooden-fenced garden were all kinds of vegetables that would grow at that altitude—carrots, parsley, turnips, peas, beets, and of course cabbage and beans. I would pull radishes from the dirt, shake them off, and eat them in the garden. The big broad beans grew as tall as me. The only thing we didn't have were lettuces for salad, which were not commonly grown in that area. But I particularly loved lettuce, and some days I would hike forty-five minutes to see if the nearest farmer had it, often to return empty-handed.

My mother, my sisters, and I would go on hikes to forage for food. We would scout out dandelion greens in the fields, watercress next to the stream, and blueberries, raspberries, and blackberries from the bushes. All of nature's treasures were just waiting to be found.

On holidays or some weekends, Vati, our father, would make the long trip from Vienna to the farm to visit us. He would arrive in his white linen hat, looking so handsome. We rarely saw him and knew nothing of his world outside the farm. Like many people in Vienna, he was doing what he had to do to survive. On the one hand, he was hiding his friend's Jewish wife and child. On the other, he was running a profitable business making safety glass for military vehicles used by the Austrian army. He was also maintaining two movie houses and part of the Prater, a famous amusement park, safeguarding those businesses for his Jewish friends who had fled during the Nazi occupation, in order to give them back after the war. Meanwhile—partly because of the atmosphere of the war, when people thought they could die at any time—he was having affairs with other women while our mother stayed with us in the mountains. But we knew none of this.

One of our favorite things to do with Vati was to go mushroom hunting. Late summer and fall is mushroom season in Tyrol, and these excursions were magical. We would lace up our hiking boots and take off into the forest, looking for chanterelles, parasols, and porcinis. Parasols were our favorites; when they were ready to be picked, they stood up straight in the pine forest, looking like umbrellas. They smelled like soil made from wildflowers. The chanterelles grew nestled between moss and pine needles, making them very difficult to find. I was never good at spotting mushrooms, but my older sisters were kind to me and would walk right past the obvious ones so that I could delight in finding them.

Later in the season, we would find porcinis, so many we couldn't eat them all at once. To preserve the porcinis, Mutti would slice them thin and then thread them with a needle and twine to hang up to dry, like baby doll laundry.

We would come back to the farm with a big basket of mushrooms and have a feast. Mutti would prepare the parasol mushrooms like Wiener schnitzel—breaded and panfried in butter. She would sauté the chanterelles or scramble them with eggs, which we would eat for dinner with rye bread and butter and some vegetables. Afterward, we would sit on the balcony, bundled up in the cold, fresh air, staring out at magnificent mountains, all of us singing loudly, despite our terrible singing voices. That was a wonderful hour, that time after dinner, watching the sunset, our stomachs filled with fresh mushrooms sautéed in butter, eaten with rye bread.

Although the war was distant, it was nonetheless always

present, with airplanes constantly flying overhead, dropping bombs as they returned home. One day, I was playing outside, splashing in our trough, which was made from a hollowed-out tree trunk, when I suddenly heard a loud rumbling noise like a faraway explosion. I instinctively ran to the other side of the house, where my mother was searching frantically for me. When I turned around, I saw that the whole side of the mountain had slid down, and the dirt from the avalanche had completely covered the area where I'd been playing. It wasn't a bomb but a landslide. Had I stayed there, I would have been buried. That moment changed me. It gave me the sense, from then on, that we have to make the most of what we have today.

The farm was my early education. I learned that no matter whether you were rich or poor, during war or peace, food was precious. Growing and producing food required unremitting work and care, with no waste. As a result, today at Restaurant Nora, I use everything: stems of vegetables for soup, livers from our chickens for pâté, pork fat compacted and sliced thin for wrapping around birds or pâtés, meat trimming scraps for stews or ground for sauces. Anything we can't compost, we put into a stock. My experience at the farm gave me the utmost respect for farmers and, I like to think, makes it easier for me to work with them directly, because I understand where good, clean food comes from and how much work it takes to produce.

On the farm, everything came directly from the earth and from our own hands. We knew what was put into the fields, the animals, the plants, and our own bodies. Today, I'm very much aware that this is where my passion for food and nature comes from. These organic foods are what make us truly alive, and it has been my life's work to communicate that passion on the plate and in the journey that has been my restaurant and my life.

CHAPTER 2

Vienna

When we returned to Vienna after the war, everything was gray. People walked around the city with their heads down, haggard and thin, disoriented and defeated. Rubble from bombed buildings was piled everywhere. The atmosphere was thick with anxiety and fear. It was just like in the film *The Third Man,* with Orson Welles; there were soldiers everywhere and people slipping in and out of shadows. Of course I was still very young, but now, when I think of that period just after the war, I picture Picasso in his Blue Period, an unrelenting feeling of bleakness and depression.

The winter of 1946–47 was particularly cold and harsh, and people struggled to survive. They had very little to eat; I recall my mother saying that it took a suitcase of money to buy a loaf of bread. People stood in lines for food, which was strictly rationed. Farmers had not been able to get back to their regular, seasonal business of planting. Just as I had learned on the farm, nothing is more precious or fundamental than food.

The desperation of the postwar situation came home to me when we found our dog Ajax, a black German shepherd, lifeless in the garden. He had been poisoned because someone didn't think it was right that a dog should have food to eat when there were people who did not have enough food to survive. I cried bitterly, because of course I had no understanding of the extent of human suffering during the war nor of how lucky we were to have come through it so unscathed.

Only later did I begin to comprehend the enormity of the war. One day, I asked my father if I was Jewish. I had dark hair, and other children frequently asked me that question at school. I didn't know what being Jewish meant. I had no idea that my childhood friend Herthi, whom we'd sheltered during the war, was Jewish.

"If you were Jewish, you probably would not be alive," he replied.

After the war, the whole of Austria, including Vienna, was divided into four zones—British, American, French, and Russian. We lived in the American section. When you traveled outside Vienna, you had to show papers if you went from one zone to another, like crossing the border to another country. My mother tried to make a game of it for us and made up stories of how the different people who occupied Vienna had different personalities. Mutti was able to make her way around easily from zone to zone because she was beautiful; everyone said she looked like Hedy Lamarr, with the same dark, wavy hair, full lips, tall slender figure, and creamy skin. The Americans offered her gum or cigarettes and complimented her on her perfect teeth. The French flirted with her, whistling and trying to pinch her on the bottom. The Russians were very friendly to us, because they loved children. The British, my mother would say with a laugh, were simply reserved and distant.

My sisters and I thought it was great fun having to show your papers to go across the occupied zones, so we made our own passports—drawing our portraits instead of using photographs, pasting them in, and writing our names. Usually, the soldiers would laugh, and some of them would even stamp our mock passports. But one time, the soldier checking papers looked furious when he saw our passports, which my mother snatched away, hurrying us in another direction. I learned that you always had to be wary, that things were often fraught with menace and you never knew how someone might react.

The atmosphere in Vienna was very different from the farm in Tyrol, which I missed terribly. There, I'd been able to run and play freely and not feel cooped up in a house or scared of soldiers and strangers. Unlike in Vienna, there had been plenty of food for everyone. I longed to be back on the farm, but Mutti said we could only go in the summer or at Christmas. We had to get back to school and to our lives from before the war.

My mother's family had lost much of their furniture and art, which had been stored in warehouses that were bombed. But we were lucky: our house stood intact, if a little worn from the Russian soldiers who had temporarily occupied it, and we were financially comfortable. So it was easier for us than most to get back to something like a normal life.

Our house was large and situated in a wonderful district in Vienna, near the *Wienerwald,* or Vienna Woods. The house was divided into four apartments; we lived on the middle floor, in what was the biggest apartment of the bunch. Years before, the emperor had made a law that Vienna couldn't expand past the woods; he thought the forest was necessary to purify the air and keep the climate steady. He was really ahead of his time. Our house was also near several vineyards, in a district known for *Heurigen,* typical Viennese taverns with gardens where you drank the wine made that year (*Heurigen* means "this year"). We lived on the same street where Beethoven had once resided, in the Eroicagasse, near the house where he composed his Symphony no. 3, *Eroica.* Actually, Beethoven lived in many houses on our street; legend has it that he never paid his rent and was so noisy and quarrelsome that he kept getting thrown out and had to move from place to place.

Ours was the largest house in the neighborhood, because it had originally been the guesthouse of a palace of a Hungarian baron. My mother's parents had given her the house as a wedding present when my parents married in 1938. In typical Viennese fashion, the house was built on a grand scale, with an enormous entrance, a sweeping marble staircase, parquet floors, and huge windows and doors. My mother, whose tastes were modern, had it decorated in Austrian Art Nouveau style, or *Jugendstil,* with sleek black lacquer furniture and red velvet upholstery and curtains. We had a large garden with fruit trees—walnut, prune, and apricot. Our cellar was stocked with jars of these fruits, so we always had extra food set aside for shortages. We even had a chicken coop that sat on the outside of the garden so that the chickens could run freely around the garden's perimeter.

My father's mother, Omi, lived upstairs in another small apartment, which had a small veranda with a beautiful view of the vineyards and mountains. It was so sunny that she grew tomato plants there. I loved to go up and visit her just to smell them.

Most of my early memories in that house are of the smells and tastes of food—in the cellar, the kitchen, and the garden. Maybe that's because unless we grew it or raised it ourselves, food was not readily available. My sisters later teased me that I remembered very little about our childhood other than what we ate! But I suppose food is a doorway into memory so that now the smell of a tomato plant in the soil brings me right back to my grandmother's veranda, with its wide view of the Vienna Woods.

As peaceful as our home was from the outside, inside things were tense. My parents had gotten married after a brief and heady romance in 1938 and then spent most of the war apart. Now they were back to the reality of living together and realizing that they had very little in common.

My mother was a glamorous tomboy from a well-to-do family. She was a living contradiction, especially for the times:

On the one hand, she was gorgeous, tall, and long-legged, with fair skin and thick auburn hair. On the other, she had no interest whatsoever in looking or behaving in a traditionally feminine manner. She was a free spirit and an intellectual who had studied first in Vienna, then in Berlin—which she described as the "Paris of the north"—to get a degree in economics. The last thing she wanted to spend her life doing was keeping house and taking care of children. But she was a creative, caring, supportive woman—and mother—who encouraged me to accomplish whatever I wanted to do and was a great influence on me. As her youngest child, I had a special bond with her.

My father came from a simpler background but had every bit as much dash. He was a businessman who loved sports and had never gone to college; at eighteen, he took over his father's glass business. He was handsome and dapper, with a chiseled face that looked nearly Greek and shiny black hair. They'd met when she whizzed by him on a motorcycle, flashing her brilliant smile. He'd swept her off her feet, and when she quickly became pregnant with Christa, they married. Otherwise, they likely would have gone their separate ways. Together, they made a handsome couple, but other than their love of the outdoors and physical activity they were worlds apart. I think my mother had truly been in love with my father—it seemed every time she came to visit Vienna during the war, she came back to the farm pregnant—but back home after the war it must have dawned on both of them that they were very different people.

Father expected Mutti to be a contented hausfrau, raising

the kids, cleaning, cooking, and having everything tidy and nice when he got home. "Kinder, Küche, Kirche" is the Austrian phrase for a woman's responsibilities: children, kitchen, church. He seemed to have forgotten how he met my mother, that she longed for adventure and was much happier on the road than at home. While Mutti liked to cook—it made her happy to create something that brought us all such pleasure, and she liked when we were all together—she hated shopping and cleaning, and having grown up with a maid, she wasn't used to handling these chores herself.

My father complained that my mother was careless about the house; when she cooked, for example, she made a total mess, using every pot. She was a terrible house cleaner, too, and while we did have a live-in maid for a while, my father's finances diminished significantly in the years after the war, and we only had a cleaning woman come once a week; still, mother did no more cleaning than when we had full-time help. Cleaning just never occurred to her. My father's mother, Omi, would join in his complaints about what a disaster my mother was as a housewife. Socially, my parents had very few shared friends. My mother loved artists and intellectuals and thought my father's business friends were all crushing bores. My father, in turn, thought all my mother's colorful acquaintances were crazy. He ended up spending a lot of time away from home—as I learned later, with other women.

Even though my father was rarely home, he, like my mother, had a huge influence on my character and on what I would become. He had a tremendous passion for the outdoors and for healthy living. His mantra, in some ways, became my own: "Health is the most important thing you have in your life, and you must take care of it. No money in the world can buy it for you." I grew up with a strong sense that you have to take pride in your body and be responsible for your own health and that what makes you healthy are the things you put in your body, the environment you surround yourself with, and the exercise you do to take care of yourself.

At the time, people probably considered my father a bit of a health nut. He was very athletic, renowned as a pole-vaulter as a young man, and able to jump easily across creeks and streams. He kept very fit, playing tennis, hiking, and skiing. He was rather short, with an elegant, trim body and skin that seemed always tan from the sun. Though he was rarely around the house, when he was, he arrived with a burst of energy. He would fling open the doors on Saturday mornings, after having played tennis, and set down big bags of fruits. I don't know where he got it all, but he splurged on oranges, bananas, grapes, apples, and beautiful peaches. It made every Saturday seem like Christmas.

My father's focus on his diet also influenced me a great deal. His eating regimen was rather strict and completely health oriented. He only ate dark, whole-grain bread, not bread made from white flour. Every morning he would drink special herbal tea he bought from the pharmacy—it was supposed to reduce stress—which he would have for breakfast with that dark bread, along with some red peppers and romaine lettuce. My mother would almost never join him at the table for breakfast;

I think their food tastes were as incompatible as everything else. My father chose to eat very simply. When I am home, I eat like my father: in the summer, some yogurt for breakfast with salsa or maple syrup, some fruits; in the winter, miso broth with tofu and a lot of vegetables.

My father was also deeply concerned with maintaining his body. Every morning he took a ten-minute shower and brushed his entire body with a big brush, to get the circulation moving. After that, he took a cold shower because he believed it helped to close his pores and prevent sickness. He regularly flossed his teeth, too, at a time when dental floss was very uncommon; it was made from duck's intestines or something similar.

Vati was convinced that in order to live healthily, it was essential to get outside and pump up your spirit and muscles with exercise, particularly during the cold and depressing winters. He felt fresh air was a tonic for the soul and often took us hiking, skiing, berry picking, or playing in the snow. What I loved most was when he took us to a hot spring outside Vienna called Baden. He believed the mineral waters were good for your body and that shocking your body with cold and hot temperatures was good for your constitution. Of course it was a special treat for us girls to go along with him to swim and splash around in the waters. We loved to loll in the sulfuric hot springs, with their rotten-egg smell.

He encouraged us in numerous directions. He certainly liked having pretty daughters, well attired in our matching coats and outfits, and hoped that we would grow up to become more conventional wives than his own; he also wanted us to learn a trade so we could be independent, if need be. He also inspired us to be athletic and outdoorsy, which had an enormous influence on me; I still love hiking, skiing, and walking in nature. He insisted that we learn to play tennis and swim and taught us to ride bicycles. He even tried to teach us to play soccer, but, alas, we girls were hopeless at it.

I suppose my father would have been happy to have a hearty son to play with, but he never let on any sense of disappointment about having three daughters in the house. When people asked how he felt about not having any sons, he crowed that he was the luckiest man in the world to have three such beautiful girls. For the precious little time that we spent with him, we still believed we were his entire world.

One of the few beliefs my parents shared, apart from the value of outdoor exercise, was the idea that you are what you eat; food is the basis for your health and is even medicine. When we were children, if we were ill, my mother prepared special foods to make us better.

For instance, when we were young, we would sometimes get worms. God knows where we got them, but we did. The cure for worms, according to my mother—and it really worked— was to eat garlic toast. She would toast some rye bread over an open flame and then rub a peeled piece of garlic against it. It was warm and spicy and absolutely delicious. I used to tell my mother I had worms all the time just so I could eat garlic toast. She must have wondered what I was up to. Or maybe she was wise to me and played along. I still love garlic toast. I put it everywhere I can, especially when I cook mussels or make a bouillabaisse or have a simple salad.

When we had upset stomachs, the remedy was to eat a porridge of cooked oatmeal mixed with grated apple. When we had sore throats, Mutti would make hot lemonade with honey. For earaches, she would mix olive oil with chopped garlic and put a drop in the ear. If we had sunburn, she would cut up slices of cucumber and tomato and place them on our sunburned skin, and the cucumber would cool the pain while somehow the acids from the tomato helped the skin heal. Because my hair was thin, my mother steeped a mixture of nettles to rinse my hair, in order to make it thicker and healthier. And of course, I was convinced that Italian gelato cured you after you had your tonsils out. I remember wishing I had another pair of tonsils to take out so I could have more gelato.

Whatever our ailment, there was some remedy in nature to heal it. I grew up believing that nature provides all the ingredients you need to heal yourself. I eat a lot of foods consciously because they are healthful. I eat cilantro because it removes mercury in the system. I eat garlic because it fights infection. I believe in homeopathy and other forms of alternative medicine, in conjunction with appropriate Western medicine, because I think we can encourage nature to help heal ourselves, which is different from bombarding our bodies with medicines that hide our symptoms and suppress our natural healing abilities. There is a lot you can do to keep yourself healthy using food and herbs.

. . .

We mainly saw Vati on the weekends; Mutti was in charge of our day-to-day lives. Because she was such an independent person herself, she gave us a fairly free hand to do what we liked. As soon as we came back to Vienna after the war, she sent us all to the French school. She'd always loved France, so she wanted us to learn the French language and culture. I think it was perhaps especially important to her, after the war, that we didn't just speak German. She wanted us to learn about different cultures and become young citizens of the world.

I loved the French school because it was housed in a big former palace with an enormous iron gate and a beautiful park on one side. Attending the school was much more difficult for my older sisters, Christa and Rosi, because the other, older children taunted them. Most of the students were the children of French, British, or American diplomats or soldiers stationed in Vienna. In school, they would scream "Losers! Losers!" at us because the Austrians were on the side that had lost the war. It bothered Christa a great deal; I was so young I was oblivious and just enjoyed myself. But Christa and Rosi felt the stigma of being losers and outsiders. In Rosi's case, that was a feeling that never really went away.

The school itself was very formal. I had to be there right on time: I was called first in roll call because my maiden name begins with an *A*—Aschenbrenner. I remember, at first, feeling terrified, because I didn't speak French well, and I had difficulties concentrating; if I were a child today, I would probably be diagnosed with a learning disability. We were supposed to memorize pages and pages of French classics like Baudelaire and Victor Hugo, which was very hard for me. But lunches, of course, are the memories that have stayed with me the longest.

Meals there were proper and very grown-up. We didn't just line up and bolt our food; we were served our food as if we were in a restaurant. The first time I sat down to lunch at the French school, I was surprised at how different it was from the way we ate at home. In Austria, you serve food as you do in the United States: when you sit down to dinner, all the food is on the table—you pile everything on your plate at once— the meat here, the vegetable there. So when, that first day, we were served just a little plate of salad, I wondered how they expected us to survive the entire afternoon on lettuce alone. I soon learned, however, that in France they serve courses, one dish sequentially after another, even in elementary school. They savor every course and make the meal last.

Every meal would start with a little appetizer. For some reason, I remember fresh radishes with sea salt and butter the best; they were so fresh and red and almost spicy. After the appetizer was removed, we would have a piece of meat with a potato, such as a piece of roast beef with French fries or another type of sauced meat with mashed potatoes. Alongside, we would have some cooked vegetables. The meal was always followed by a dessert, whether it was a piece of fruit, a small piece of cake, a wedge of cheese, or a piece of chocolate. That was the conclusion to our luncheon ritual.

It was important, in French school, to learn how to behave

well at the table. We sat at our places and learned how to use a knife and a fork correctly and how to have good table manners. We had to do everything properly, from placing our napkins in our laps before the meals to peeling an orange for dessert with a knife and a fork. More than just learning how to eat in a nice manner, we learned how to make conversation with others at the table—how to be friendly and inclusive of others, how to be diplomatic, and how to be polite to the waitresses. This was a huge lesson to me: Food isn't just to feed yourself; it is also a social activity. You don't just nourish your body; you nourish the company you keep.

At the beginning of the school year, you were able to choose your table and the group of children you were to eat with for the rest of the year. I was not the most popular child—I was not French but Austrian, and I was a little more reclusive—I wasn't the best student, and it was difficult to make friends. When the bell rang on that first day, we rushed into the dining room to seek out our seats. What I learned, however, was that it was most important to choose not by the other students but by the waitress; she needed to be fast, treat you well, and give you seconds if you wanted them! During lunch, you were then forced to make conversation with kids whom you might not be friends with, but as time passed, and over conversations, you realized that actually you did like them. So the art of social conversation was essential here, too.

I wish that every child could learn to eat the way I learned at the French school. Good food and a relaxed atmosphere make for life's most pleasant moments—an atmosphere that

I have tried to create in my restaurants and in my home. It's so important that people pay attention to their food and treat mealtimes with respect. Learning to eat properly is an essential part of a child's education. These early lessons of taking time in life to sit down to eat simple, healthy foods, prepared with care, were never lost on me.

My mother didn't mind that I wasn't an outstanding student. She had it in her head that I should be the artistic one in the family, so in addition to French school she sent me to dancing school. Like my father, she believed that it was of utmost importance to keep your body healthy, and so they were eager from the start to have me dance.

My mother, though she didn't have exactly the same beliefs as my father, really embraced the idea of cooking healthfully—a lighter kind of food, as opposed to the heavy roux and sauces that were more traditional to Viennese cooking. She loved to ski and hike and to spend time outdoors; she was a curious, adventurous soul.

I don't think she thought I would become a prima ballerina, but more of a modern or jazz dancer; she imagined me as another Ginger Rogers, spinning around with Fred Astaire. She never pushed me too hard, but she felt that dancing would give me another interesting direction in life.

I loved to dance—I still do—but the training schedule was grueling. Starting from the age of four, I had six hours a week of dance lessons—ballet, modern, and some sort of gymnastics. I was so exhausted when I came home from school that I couldn't even bathe myself. But dance is where I learned what became essential to me later in life, which is to have discipline and creativity in equal measure.

It was during dance lessons that I realized I have an imagination. I would create whole dance scenes in my head, like stories. It was also when I understood that I had to have the strength and discipline to keep going even when I felt tired. It's important to know that you have the resources when you are exhausted to keep going and not give up; it gives you a sense of personal strength and accomplishment. Those lessons also helped me later in life as a chef, starting my own restaurant, when you have to have the discipline to get up early to do your work every day, stand on your feet all day, stay until long after the last diner leaves—and continue to be creative.

I stopped rigorous dance training when I was fourteen, the age when young dancers had to go full-time to the dance academy and give up their scholastic lives. The truth was that I was never going to be a star: I was too short, the teacher told me my neck wasn't long enough, and while I was good, I was not brilliant. Also, I had frostbitten my toes once when I was iceskating and so could not dance on toe shoes. In some ways, it was a relief to stop. I no longer had to constantly worry about whether I would injure myself. Because dancing had always come first, I'd never been allowed to ski competitively or do anything else athletic that might injure me. Now I was finally free to take control of my own body and didn't have to worry about my weight or anything else.

But to this day, I love to dance. Wherever there's music, I like to dance, and when I give a party, I always have music for dancing. Dancing is a very important part of life; it's exciting to see how you move with a partner and how he expresses himself through his movements and rhythm. It's also wonderful with friends, to dance and just let your body go, expressing itself to the sound. I have always taken dance classes, not only to keep in shape, but to stay happy. There's no better way to feel free and joyful in your body.

After I stopped going to formal dance classes, I was home more in the afternoons and spent more time with my mother. I would sit with her in the kitchen and talk to her about my day while I watched her cook. I became completely absorbed in the way she turned ingredients into a finished meal. She never encouraged me to help; I picked up cooking by observing. Those afternoons cooking were our most intimate time together and gave me a sense of how preparing food brings people together.

I would often sit at the table and watch her make our favorite dish, Wiener schnitzel. She would take veal cutlets, make tiny incisions in them to prevent them from curling when they fried, and pound them between two sheets of wax paper until they were only a quarter-inch thin. Then she'd season them and give them a dusting of flour. She'd dip the cutlets in an egg-and-milk mixture, then bread crumbs, patting them on each side so they'd adhere. Then she'd heat a cast-iron pan with about an inch of vegetable oil. She would test if the oil was hot enough by throwing a piece of bread in the pan to see if it would sizzle and turn a golden brown. When it was ready, she would fry the cutlets quickly and serve them with a little parsley and a wedge of lemon. Her Wiener schnitzel was absolutely delicious—crispy and never greasy. It was heavenly.

Mutti often made a traditional potato salad to serve with the Wiener schnitzel. I can smell it today: tarragon and green onions or chives. She used little waxy fingerling potatoes, not the floury type you use to make mashed potatoes. First, she would boil them in their skins until they were tender, peel them while they were still steaming hot, and slice them thinly. Then she'd pour a dressing over the potatoes—tarragon vinegar and some peanut oil, I think—and the whole salad would become creamy without any mayonnaise or cream.

Mutti made a lot of salads. I loved her cucumber salad with lots of garlic and sweet paprika and her Boston lettuce salads. She used romaine leaves as the Austrians do, as "cooking salad," where she cut them into half-inch shreds, sautéed them with a little onion until they wilted, then dusted them lightly with flour and added some stock, which made what was, fundamentally, a very thin béchamel with cooked greens. Most of her cooking was very light. She taught me the basics of cooking and how to prepare great-tasting food easily. From Mutti, I learned that you don't have to slave over the stove for hours in order to eat well.

The most special salad Mutti made was the Christmas salad. It made me very excited when she started to make this salad, because that meant Christmas was coming. Every year, my mother's mother would come visit, and they would make the Christmas salad, cooking together all day long. Grosse Omi, as we called her, was rather eccentric; she was a large, slovenly woman, a gambler who'd lost a lot of money and then became a kind of hoarder, buying odd objects and regularly carrying them around with her in a big bag. While my mother liked having us watch her in the kitchen, Grosse Omi was not so welcoming. My mother was not an affectionate woman, and it's clear, from watching Grosse Omi, that this was a result of the emotionally cold household in which she grew up. Every time we came into the kitchen, Omi would begin speaking in what we called *B-Sprache*—the German equivalent of pig Latin—so that we wouldn't understand; we thought it was a different language.

Still, I loved to watch them make the Christmas salad. They would get all kinds of root vegetables—carrots, beets, parsnips, celery root—and cook them separately, then dice them into little squares. Then they would make a mustardy mayonnaise, chop some dill pickles, and mix it all together with some cooked lentils. The whole thing would turn bright pink because of the beets. It's impossible to describe the taste—it was tangy and earthy and a little sweet—but it was wonderful, and to me it tasted like Christmas.

This salad was just one of Mutti's preparations for Christmas, which was such a special day. It was so exciting to wake up early in the morning and fling open the doors of the living room to see our tree—nearly twenty feet high—which she'd

trimmed with real candles and decorated with all edible orna-
ments: meringues, chocolates, and gingerbread men. We could
just about eat our way through the tree until January. We would
sing Christmas carols together and open presents, and in the
afternoon we'd have a special meal of "Indian," as we called
it (or "turkey," as the rest of us know it), because my mother
didn't like to cook the carp that was a traditional Christmas
meal. The elaborate effort my mother put into Christmas for
us children made up for the fact that my father never gave any
of us presents; I don't remember him ever giving me one in my
entire life, actually. He'd probably say his best present was taking care of us by going to work every day and providing for us.

Mutti wasn't the only person I liked to watch cook. After
the war, my parents rented out the apartment downstairs to
another family. The tenant, Frau Thomas, was the daughter
of a restaurant owner, and she cooked a lot. My mother was
a good cook, but with the exception of the holiday feasts she
was more interested in quick, healthy meals and convenience;
we always had to have the new appliances that made cooking
faster. But Frau Thomas, unlike my mother, made cooking an
art.

On Saturdays, I would sneak downstairs to watch her. It got
to the point where she would expect me. I'd sit in the kitchen
and look after her baby while she cooked. She was patient and
methodical in the kitchen and cooked many dishes that took
a lot of time—long braises that took all morning, elaborate

veal-bone broths, which ended up clear, light, and flavorful. She also made different soups from scratch, cutting all manner of vegetables and throwing them into a big pot.

I particularly loved watching Frau Thomas bake traditional Austrian cakes and especially strudel. She would mix the dough with quick, practiced hands until it was a perfect, slightly elastic consistency. Then she spread her big table with a towel and sprinkled flour on it. She'd place the dough in the middle and stretch it with her fingers, like a pizza, until it was hanging over the table. When she pulled the dough, it was paper-thin; you could read through it. Then she sprinkled the dough with sliced apples, raisins, walnuts, cinnamon, sugar, and pats of butter. She carefully rolled it up from one side, like a jelly roll, and brushed it with more butter. She baked it—the cinnamon smell was heavenly!—until it was nice and crispy on the outside but the apples were still a little crunchy on the inside. Austria is famous for its strudel, of course, and she was a master. She'd make poppy seed strudel, cheese strudel, and even savory strudels with cabbage.

My mother didn't like it when I went down to watch the neighbor cook. I think it made her feel lonely, because cooking was our special time together. I sometimes regret that I didn't use that time to be with her, to ask her more questions about herself and about things I didn't understand. Some part of me realized that she was unhappy. Occasionally, when my father was home, she would cry and run out of the room and hide in her bedroom.

I clearly remember them fighting over getting a dishwasher. Dishwashers were uncommon and very expensive. My mother tried to wheedle my father into one, but he wouldn't relent. He thought it was ridiculous that a woman would need a machine to wash dishes. "Just break the plates," my father roared. "Just use them once and break them. That will cost less than a dishwasher!" But eventually—perhaps because she borrowed the money from her family—my mother had a dishwasher installed in the kitchen.

My sisters and I knew that my parents had an unhappy marriage, but no matter what their troubles, Mutti never said anything bad about my father to us, even though he criticized her constantly and ran around with other women. She knew he had other women; it's very European to accept that your husband has a mistress, and maybe the wife has lovers, too. I suppose that's why I accepted men who cheated on me later in life; it's simply what I learned from my parents. In any case, my mother believed that you don't take your children's admiration away from their father by putting him down. We knew they were not happy together and wondered why they did not divorce.

I must have been around twelve when I noticed that my parents didn't sleep in the same room anymore. My father said it was because he liked to sleep in the cold; he slept on the veranda because there were no more spare bedrooms.

My French teacher took a liking to me and told me he saw my father with another woman. I told my grandmother, who told my father, and from then on he was more careful to keep it hidden from us.

One time, I did get the nerve to ask Mutti why she stayed with Vati. She told me that she had actually gone to a lawyer once, who told her that if she tried to divorce him, she would never get to keep the children. She could get divorced, but she would walk away empty-handed. Not only that, but people looked down on the children of divorced parents at the time, and she didn't want us to suffer that stigma. She loved us and felt she owed it to us to stick around.

Until I was a teenager, my sisters, for the most part, treated me like the baby, basically ignoring me. When I was thirteen, Christa was eighteen and Rosi was fifteen, and they preferred to go out with their friends, to clubs and dances. They didn't have much time for me until I developed an interest in clothes, boys, and going out dancing, too.

My sister Christa was my father's darling. Christa was curvy, petite, and very attractive. She and my mother never got on well; maybe my mother resented that she'd had to get married because she was pregnant with Christa, but in any case there was often some tension between them. Christa, like my father, reproached my mother for not being a good housewife or an attentive mother and for not dressing what she thought of as appropriately. All those things were important to Christa. She later went to design school and became a master seamstress; she taught me early how to dress to be chic, and like her I love fashion and beautiful clothes. But Christa struggled with my mother, who was such a tomboy.

Rosi, like many middle children, had the toughest role in the family. As a child, she suffered terrible allergies and ear infections, and she spent quite a bit of time in the hospital, alone, while we were on the farm, when she was only five years old. She might have died during that time, had it not been for the penicillin brought by the Americans helping in the hospitals. She wasn't as outgoing as Christa and had more of a brooding, introspective personality. She was tall and slim, with my father's aristocratic long nose. For many years, I was closest to her.

For a brief period, we were inseparable. On the weekends, we would give ourselves face masks, take care of our hair, and set out the clothes we wanted to wear during the evening. Christa would show me how to put on makeup, and she would sew beautiful clothes for us. She could sew anything; I remember my father gave her his old tweed suit, and she made it into a wonderful little pencil skirt and jacket. I suppose I'm that way with food; I can look into what seems like an empty fridge and make a good meal. We all learned to do a lot with very little.

One Christmas, when I was about fifteen, my whole family went on a vacation, skiing in Kitzbühel. The ski resort was situated in a small, medieval town in Tyrol, which was beautiful in winter, the stone building sparkling with an icing of snow. We girls loved to ski—though I was not a competitive skier like my sisters—but we also loved the social life around the resort. We were somewhat notorious in Kitzbühel for being glamorous, because we skied well and in the evenings we dressed up and could dance well. My sisters and I always made sure we looked good; we knit thick ski sweaters, which we used like anoraks, from wool that we had dyed in vibrant colors that would match our ski pants. The pants were so tight we needed someone else to close our skis because we could barely bend down. But we looked great on the slopes. I don't even think we wore goggles or hats because we thought they'd spoil the look.

Usually, we would ski until lunch and then go to one of the little log cabins on the slopes, where the shepherds stayed in the summer and which in the winter they made into dining rooms. Everyone sat around big wooden tables and benches and ate simple food cooked on a woodstove by the shepherd's wife. We'd have goulash or green pea soup and my favorite dish there, *Kaiserschmarrn,* which means "the emperor's nothing." It must have been invented by someone who had a lot of mishaps with an omelet, because basically you beat a lot of eggs together, add sugar and a little flour and raisins, and then fry them in butter, turn it, then tear it with two forks and serve it with powdered sugar and a compote of prunes or apples.

After lunch, we'd ski again until four o'clock and then rush back to our rooms to get ready for the five o'clock tea. We quickly changed from our ski clothes, fixed our hair and makeup, and then went back to the lodge, where we sat around drinking tea and socializing, hoping to be asked to dance or to dinner. My mother joined us as a chaperone, because it wouldn't have been proper for us to hang out there by ourselves.

One afternoon, at one of the teas, my sisters and I noticed

a handsome young man looking over at our table. I was certain he was looking at my sisters, not at me; I was young and small and thought no one noticed me.

But to my surprise, he came over, performed a little bow in front of me, and asked me to dance. I was astonished—and absolutely frozen in place. My sisters shook their heads—the youngest getting asked to dance first!—but they pushed me to dance with him. He looked a bit older than me and very confident, so I was nervous, but I forgot that, because the music and dancing, and the stories he told me about himself, swept me away.

After the dance, I found out that his name was Aki—short for Alexander—and he, too, was from Vienna. He was seventeen, in his last year of high school, and incredibly handsome and elegant. He asked me if he could meet me the next day at the hut on the slopes. From then on, we spent all our time together on vacation and began to see each other back in Vienna. For our first date in Vienna, he took me to listen to music in a nightclub, a sultry place with a very Marlene Dietrich feeling. I was thrilled and felt so grown up.

My parents were happy for me to have a boyfriend but cautioned me about not behaving properly. "In my eyes, you're a grown-up now, and you're responsible for what happens to you," my father told me. That made a big impression on me.

It turned out that Aki came from an aristocratic family; his father was a count. My family was comfortable—upper-middle class, I suppose, though we were always careful with money—but his was truly a different class, old money. None of that mattered to Aki, though. He loved to be with me and to take me out. To me, he was so sophisticated; he knew everything about the theater and literature and all the places to go out in Vienna. I think part of what he liked about me was that I was different from the girls he was used to. I was game for anything—skiing, hiking. I liked to dress up and look pretty, but I was also happy to go outdoors and have fun.

I had plenty of other friends, but Aki was the one who showed me a completely different side of Vienna, the Vienna of glittering cafés, balls, and swanky music clubs. I was enchanted. My family never went to restaurants; we ate at home, unless we were traveling, and then we had simple, hearty Austrian food. My only experience with anything approaching fine dining was eating lunch at the French school.

But Vienna, of course, has a long history of beautiful cafés and restaurants. The center of town is filled with *Konditoreien* (pastry shops) and *Kaffeehäuser* (cafés) showcasing elaborate pastries. One of the cafés Aki took me to was the famous Sacher Café. The Sacher was marvelous, all upholstered in velvet, with red walls, big gold-framed portraits, crystal chandeliers, and marble-topped bistro tables—a place fit for a princess. When you walked in, you felt as if the war had never happened and you were living the high life during the Hapsburg Empire. It was thrilling to be served by the waiters, who were so dressed up and polite, and to be able to choose from such an extensive menu.

I remember clearly what we had: the famous *Tafelspitz*, which is incredibly tender, slowly boiled beef, like a brisket, served on a plate with applesauce and horseradish, small boiled potatoes rolled in butter with some chopped parsley on top, and some creamed spinach. I wasn't much of a drinker, but the wine Aki ordered made me swoon. I remember it was a Nuits-Saint-George, and I thought it was the best thing I had ever tasted. I had thought most Austrian wine was too sour for me, and so French wine was a revelation.

The whole meal led up to the Sacher torte, which may be the most famous dessert in Austria. It's layered chocolate sponge cake with apricot jam, glazed in chocolate, served with unsweetened whipped cream. It's not too sweet, and the apricots play off the dark chocolate perfectly. As any Viennese person can tell you, the cake was invented by Franz Sacher, the father of the founder of the Hotel Sacher, in 1832.

Going out with Aki was a whirlwind. I felt like a princess for the evening in a grand ballroom filled with elegant people. Aki introduced me to bars and clubs; we entered a realm of society and culture that I had never seen before. He took me to the theater and concerts and gave me books to read, but most important of all was the time we spent going to restaurants, where I was introduced to great food and wonderful wine.

From Aki, I learned so much about both Viennese and French cuisine. We'd also eat at Hungarian restaurants, or we'd end a long night of dancing at wonderful sausage stands. Once, for brunch, he took me to a beautiful restaurant overlooking all of Vienna, where we had hot chocolate and pastries. I'm sure I developed my love of fine dining from those wonderful experiences. I love the idea that people who come into Restaurant Nora feel transformed and that they are having a special, magical night like those I had with Aki when I was a girl.

Aki and I broke up when I was eighteen, after we were together for three years. My poor behavior at a party precipitated the breakup.

I was moody partly because I had been spending time with a friend, Mischi, who was a little wild. She drank and did too many drugs. She taught me to smoke cigarettes, partly to lose weight—even though I didn't have a weight problem—and then she gave me pharmaceutical drugs, uppers and downers. I got into a habit of taking them and even faked a prescription once to get more. I got hooked on amphetamines; I had lots of energy and lost weight, and for a good three years I took them regularly. But I was losing my sense of balance, to the point where, when Aki broke up with me, he told me that he didn't understand me anymore, that my moods were so uneven, and that he was leaving. After he left, I realized the drugs were making me unstable and not myself; I couldn't stand being dependent on them anymore. I was starting to lose my sense of myself.

This was the breaking point for me. I realized I'd let it go too far. Not long afterward, another friend and I threw them all into the gutter. That was the last time I took those kinds of drugs. That part of my life was over.

I was eighteen and had finished high school. My father thought I should learn something practical; he believed that all three of us sisters should learn a trade so we could be independent. I enrolled in a *Handelsakademie*, a sort of trade school, learning typing and shorthand, but I thought I wanted to study interior design, which is much more difficult in Austria than in the United States. I needed a year of math to be accepted into university, which I undertook, and then I got sidetracked into computer science, which was just beginning, but I was assured that computers were a man's field, so in the end I didn't pursue that line of study. The only other thing that interested me while I was in school was our off-site visits, for example, when we went to factories, like the bread factory. I loved to see things created from scratch.

But I was restless. I wanted something else from my life. I'd had a taste of fine living and food, and I had an appetite for more. Where I would find it, and how, I had no idea.

CHAPTER 3

European Travels

One day, when I was about fourteen, my mother pulled up in front of the house in a secondhand Volkswagen Bug. She was clearly very excited about the little moss-green car, which was evidently all hers. My mother had never been allowed to drive my father's Fiat convertible and could only occasionally go out with the chauffeur. Now she'd gone out and bought her own car and could drive whenever, wherever she pleased. Mutti loved to travel, and this was her getaway vehicle.

Rosi and I were excited, too. We knew how dearly Mutti wanted the freedom to travel, and we were eager to accompany her. Rosi and I were old enough to go along (Christa was already off on her own), and we couldn't wait to head out on an adventure.

The car, although used and very basic, was a treasure to us. We opened the front door and pushed forward the front seat. In back, we saw a strange metal contraption. Mutti, pleased with herself, explained that she'd had the car fixed up so that it could be turned into a kind of camper. Ingeniously, she'd designed a folding metal frame to replace the backseat and had a blacksmith build it for her. She'd covered the frame with a folded foam mattress, which we could remove and set up as a double bed. She'd also had a big patchwork tent made to pitch in camping spots. Everything was tucked away and organized, ready for travel.

My father, who only liked to stay in the best hotels, would never have spent a minute in Mutti's bohemian tent, but that was partly why she liked it: her VW camper was all hers and gave her some much-needed freedom from her confined life as a hausfrau in an indifferent marriage. Nor could my father complain, as their finances grew increasingly tight—the competition in his industry in reconstructed Germany was putting him out of business, as he couldn't compete with the new machinery the Germans had for glassmaking—that my mother was squandering money on travel if she did it gypsy-style. Mutti's Bug opened up the world for her—and us—to explore.

On our first big trip, we drove across the border to Italy, to Sistiana, a seaside village in the Friuli region, not far from Trieste. We arrived at a wide beach on the bay, surrounded by rocky cliffs, with fishing boats swaying out at sea. It was summer, and the water was clear and inviting. My mother found a prime location for our tent, right on the beach, and to our delight we were able to reserve it for the entire season. After we erected the tent, swept it out inside, and set up the bed with an air mattress next to it, we found we'd made a surprisingly comfortable little home. As soon as the tent was up, I changed into my swimsuit, ran into the water, swam out, and floated on my back, looking up at all that blue, forgetting about school, boyfriends, dance classes—everything but the bliss of that seemingly endless stretch of summer.

There was almost nothing for us to do but swim and tan ourselves on the beach—what the Italians call *dolce far niente,* or the "sweetness of doing nothing." We did, however, have meals to prepare. The best of those we made right from the ocean.

Mutti showed us how to dive for mussels, which attached themselves to the rocks at the edges of the bay. She explained that we should never take any mussels that had been exposed to the air but instead collect them underwater. We would dive, pluck the shells from the rocks, and surface again, throwing them in a bucket filled with ocean water. When we had a good quantity, we would scrape away the beards and then put them in a pot on our small camping stove. Usually, we would add chopped tomato, olive oil, and garlic to the water. We'd steam them in seawater until they opened up and eat them, juices dripping, with *panini* bread drizzled with olive oil, along with some salad. The mussels were fresh and tasted like the sea.

We ate very simply in Italy but very well. Each day, we would put on our sandals and skirts and walk to the village to shop for what we needed just for that day. It seems we lived on crusty bread, mortadella sausage, tomatoes, peaches—such sweet, fuzzy peaches!—and green salads. My mother would buy Chianti wine in a basket and sip that in the evening. I was impressed with how different this food was from anything we could get in Austria—so colorful and delicious.

The specialty food shops amazed me, too. My mother just loved olives, and in Sistiana there was a shop that sold only olives. She was in heaven, trying all the different varieties. The first time I had them I didn't like them: the smell was so acidic and astringent, and the taste was too strong for me. I was disappointed after my mother's description, but of course I eventually came to love olives, too.

Then there was a cheese shop, where, again, they sold only cheese. The smell of all those parmesans and gorgonzolas at once was overwhelming; it made me feel nearly woozy. The salesman asked my mother not only what kind of cheese we wanted but how ripe—the firm gorgonzola, the middle, or the gorgonzola dolce. I was astonished, because in Austria you have mostly firm cheeses—nothing runny or soft—and no one ever sold them by their ripeness.

The vegetable vendor took the same sort of care with her produce. When we approached her shop, with its shiny displays of bright vegetables, and asked, in our rudimentary Italian, for tomatoes, she launched into a barrage of questions we could barely understand. Tomatoes, okay, she would say, but for what? For pasta or for salad? If it's salad, you buy the hard, barely red tomatoes. For sauce, the ripe, red, fragrant, soft tomatoes. Then there was the question of when we were going to eat them—today or tomorrow? For the vegetable vendor, getting the perfect tomato was a kind of science and made me appreciate eating a vegetable at its peak ripeness for the dish you want to make. We went through that litany of questions with every fruit or vegetable we bought. Nothing was more important than getting perfect produce.

Sometimes we would shower at the campsite, put on dresses and comb our hair, and go to a local restaurant for dinner. That was an adventure in itself, because the car had no backseat now that it was being used as a bed. We would sometimes haul the air mattress into the back so it wouldn't hurt to drive over the bumpy dirt roads while we sat on the floor of the VW. We went to the local restaurants, which, because we were near the ocean, specialized in seafood. I ordered fried calamari, which you ate with your fingers, dipping the crusty rounds into aioli. We usually had salad with it, which in Italy was quite simple compared with the salads we made in Austria: rough lettuce, crunchy greens, with olive oil, red wine vinegar, and just a little salt and pepper. But the olive oil was so wonderful; it was an utter luxury in Austria, something we rarely had, and I much preferred it to the peanut or corn oil we dressed our salads with at home. That seemed to sum up Italy: everything simple was luxurious.

Those were wonderful days. We'd swim out to rocks that made a little island off the shore and tan ourselves, slathered in suntan lotion we made from olive oil with iodine and a little lemon juice. It was probably the time I felt closest to my mother, who infected me with her bohemian spirit of travel and adventure. In the evenings, as the sun went down, we would prepare our rustic meals, savoring the beauty of the beach, the sunset, and the pleasure of one another's company.

Our trips to the beach weren't the only travels we made growing up, but those times with my mother were very special. As a family, traveling had always been important; it fit in with my parents' belief that fresh mountain air is good for your well-being. In the summers we'd go hiking, and in the winters we would ski in Kitzbühel in Tyrol, then later in Zell am See, in Salzburg, the place where I eventually inherited a house from my mother and now ski with my own children and their families.

But other than those outdoor trips, it was usually my mother who took us on vacation; my father preferred to go on vacation by himself, and so it was often just me, my sisters, and Mutti. After that first trip to Italy, we went back several times. Italy seemed more elemental than Austria, close to the earth and the sea. I have another memory of staying in a pensione by the beach. We watched the *mattanza*, the killing of the tuna, when the big fish ran, and the fishermen would bring them back to shore in nets to kill and process them. The beautiful beach became a bloodbath, and the local people made a festival of the fish. For them, it was a big event; they weren't just killing the fish but paying homage to nature. (But to this day, the vivid memories of the ocean turning bloodred have kept me from wanting to swim in it.)

As we got a little older, my sisters and I were mostly interested in going to Italy to shop. My sister Christa loved the fabrics, which she would turn into wonderful creations. I loved the shoes; Austrian shoes were hard and clunky, while Italian shoes were chic and comfortable. Of course, we dashed to see museums and churches in the towns, but at that age, I'm embarrassed to say, we preferred shopping to culture. At the border, on our return, we were supposed to declare everything we'd bought. But we had a system down. We would hide the fabrics we'd bought under our skirts, and the shoes we'd bought under the seats, and then make ourselves look neglected, as if we'd just come from camping, covering ourselves in bread crumbs. The customs inspector would stick his head in the car and ask if we had anything to declare, and we'd pull out the cheapest bracelets and beach sandals we'd bought at the market, showing them off like treasures, and he'd wave us through.

Christa—petite, blond, and voluptuous—was a magnet for Italian men. We went to Florence once, and a stylish Italian named Paolo fell madly in love with her. He took us out to Italian restaurants. I was familiar with eating different courses from French school, but the Italian system was a bit different. We learned this our first time out with Paolo. We loved pasta, so we ordered big plates of it—plain spaghetti with olive oil and very ripe tomatoes cooked down to a thick sauce, then topped with a perfect cheese, whether slivers of pecorino or shards of parmesan. When we'd finished everything, they asked what we wanted as a main course; pasta was only an appetizer. We couldn't imagine eating any more! The Italians were friendly and laughed at us. I would have been happy to eat more, if I could, and thought it was a terrible shame I was so full I could only pick at the delicious-smelling veal scallopini with capers and lemon zest, which was something I could never get back home. In Austria, veal was mostly Wiener schnitzel, breaded and fried. I knew that when I got home from Italy, I would still be thinking about our wonderful meals.

In addition to all the traveling I did with my mother and sisters, I was an exchange student in high school. My older sisters had been exchange students in England and France and had had a wonderful time. My mother believed strongly that her children should learn to speak languages, both English and French, so at age twelve, in 1955, off to England I went. I was excited to go, all on my own, but from the moment I arrived, my dreams about the rolling English countryside with thatched stone cottages were deflated. I was miserable. To me, England was cold and dreary, and the family I was staying with lived in nondescript suburbs. I felt uncomfortable with them from the start. They weren't as accustomed to being outdoors and active as I had been; they spent a lot of time watching television and staying inside. No one asked me much about myself or my family or seemed curious about me. The daughter seemed particularly joyless; all she wanted to do was walk to the corner store and buy candy. The air was fraught with tension, which I was at a loss to explain, but it somehow felt focused on me.

I didn't know what to do in the situation, so I comforted myself by eating. I threw myself into food: toast, cornflakes,

Cadbury chocolate, and Wall's ice cream all day long. I put on so much weight that I decided I was pregnant; I had no idea how babies were made, but my French teacher had kissed me before I left, and I decided that because of his kiss I'd become pregnant. Finally, my host mother called up the agency and told them she didn't want me to stay anymore; she was tired of taking care of me and tired of the fact that her daughter and I didn't get along. Needless to say, this came as a shock. It wasn't quite the cultural experience I was expecting.

The agency sent me to another family in the seaport area of Chatham: a sailor and his wife, who had a daughter about my age. They weren't very well-to-do, but unlike the first family they made me feel welcome right away. The wife was a real character—big and bosomy, constantly enveloping me in hugs, pressing me up against her housedress with real affection. She usually had a Player's cigarette dangling from one corner of her mouth; she even talked with the cigarette there. Every day, she cooked savory pies. She would make a sauce with kidneys, beef, and lamb and cover it with a thick piecrust. She had a little glass bird that she would place in the pie, on top of the meat but under the crust, which prevented the dough from hitting the sauce, which seemed so clever. She was wonderful to me; she was so very kind. I admired how the wife was able to make anything and was so generous, despite their limited means. She even made me an authentic kilt to wear, folding the fabric in tight pleats so that when I sat down, I felt as if I were on a cushion. She took me to pick out the fabric, and I chose a horrible yellow pattern, and that was my parting keepsake. I got along well with the daughter, too, who had a lively, raucous imagination—she had a collection of magazines starring mainly naked women—and I was sorry when I had to say good-bye to the sailor's family.

When I arrived back home, my mother was shocked, as I had put on ten pounds in a short time. It taught me, later, something about what happens when you eat from boredom and don't spend enough time outside. I was happy to get back to my routine of dancing, hiking, skiing, and eating healthy food. I hadn't made the connection, at that point in time, that eating junk food nonstop wasn't good for me—that it affected how I looked and how I felt—and afterward I never forgot it.

As much as my mother loved the summers camping on Italian beaches, she wanted to push on to ever more exotic places. We visited Italy several times, as well as Yugoslavia. At the time, Greece seemed very remote—scarcely visited by foreigners. Of course, my mother wanted to explore. Rosi and I went with her; by this time, Christa had met her future husband and traveled with him. The rough trip ahead of us probably wouldn't have appealed much to our fashionable sister, anyway.

One summer, we loaded up the VW Bug and set out for Greece, which is a two-day trip from Austria. There weren't many highways; we had to wind our way down through the Balkans on two-lane roads. We spent a week at the Club Med on the Peloponnese thinking that we'd get acclimated to Greece. I loved having the option of a French breakfast of café au lait and croissants or a Greek breakfast of yogurt, pita bread, feta cheese, olives, and tomatoes, as well as figs and other delicious fruits. After a week, we drove on to Athens to see the impressive Acropolis and other ancient sites.

Away from Club Med, Greece felt completely alien; we didn't speak the language, and we felt out of place in the barren landscape, filled with fields of olive trees. We were too nervous even to ask for food in the stores because we couldn't speak a word of Greek. Instead, we saw watermelons being sold along the road, and so we lived on melons for days until one of us had the nerve to go to a store and start pointing at bread, yogurt, and cheese.

We traveled around villages and ended up going to Thebes. By the time we arrived, it was late, and we hadn't found a hotel. It turned dark, and everything looked boarded up. We ended up driving out of town into a field, where we camped by the car.

I woke up to the sound of bells in the morning, opened my eyes, and was startled to see an old woman staring at me. She was the oldest person I'd ever seen, dressed all in black, with a scarf around her head and a very wrinkled face. She was guarding a flock of sheep, and behind her were other women who looked like her—a flock of crows—just staring at us. My mother and my sister also woke up, and we felt like intruders, so we hurried back into the car and drove off. We decided to head straight back to Austria.

Although our Greek trip had been strange, by the time we got back to Austria, we were laughing at our adventures. Like my mother, I loved immersing myself into a strange new place, trying the local food, and understanding something about a different culture—whether it was the Greeks' different attitude toward women, who definitely seemed to be treated as a lower class than men, or their architecture, landscape, and history. I like to think that my mother's adventurous spirit, and her curiosity about other cultures, are two of my best inheritances.

After I graduated from high school, Rosi and I decided that we would take a trip together to celebrate by ourselves. My mother went along with our scheme, although I think she felt a little sad that her girls were going off on an adventure without her. But we were eighteen and twenty-one, and we wanted a taste of the kind of freedom that my mother had always enjoyed on her own on the road, but this time we wanted to do it without her.

Our plan was to go deep into Yugoslavia, which had just recently been opened to tourism. We'd been up north before, on the coast, but never ventured farther south. Like Mutti, we wanted to see new corners of the world. The country had an optimistic feeling—the Dubrovnik Airport had just opened that year, 1962, and tourists were being welcomed with open arms—so Rosi wanted to go there. My mother drove us in the VW down to Rijeka, a seaport, from which we would set off on a boat. She waved good-bye to us as the boat pulled away from the port, no doubt wishing she was on board with us.

We went below deck to our cabin, which had only a tiny porthole and was hot and muggy, with a moldy smell. It was a long way from being a cruise ship. We tried to sleep, but it was too uncomfortable, so after a while we went up on deck for fresh air.

We enjoyed the breeze and the stars until we both began to have an uncomfortable feeling. We looked around and realized that there were no other women on the deck; they were all men who looked like pirates to us, in their good-looking way, with dark hair and intense dark eyes. We felt we were being watched—which we were. We realized that traveling by ourselves was going to be different from traveling with our mother; we were no longer chaperoned, and men regarded us in a different way. We gathered up our blankets and went back below deck to that miserable, stuffy cabin to try to sleep.

When we arrived in Dubrovnik, we took a cab to our hotel on the outskirts of town, relieved finally to be in a nice room by ourselves. The room had a balcony overlooking the ocean, which was stunning; the coast in Yugoslavia has enormous rocks spilling down into the ocean, with the water smashing against the cliffs. But that night, as we were trying to sleep, we heard noises outside. We drew the curtains to look and were shocked to find men standing on our balcony, clamoring to get inside the room. They were telling us that because it was a socialist country, we had to go out with them. We called reception and finally the men left, but we were feeling ever more vulnerable and uncertain that it was a good idea to go off traveling to Yugoslavia alone.

Despite all the men trailing us, we loved Yugoslavia. The Hotel Neptun, set on the cliffs of the Dalmatian coast, was stunning, and every day we went out to sunbathe and read. We were ignoring the men altogether until one day we saw a tall, handsome man with curly hair leaning against the railing that ran along the cliffs, observing us through dark sunglasses and smoking a thin brown cigarillo, a smile playing on his lips. He looked very elegant—tan, thin, with a Bourbon nose. He seemed very sophisticated.

The man appeared to be keeping an eye on us, but he didn't come up to us, as the Yugoslavian men had. He left us alone, which only increased our curiosity about him. Rosi insisted that we go up and introduce ourselves, but I was far too shy. "I'm going to meet him," she said, brushing herself off and heading in his direction. I watched as they talked and nodded and gestured, and I wondered what they were saying.

Rosi took her time getting back to me. "Who is he?" I demanded.

"He's French and seems very nice." Already, Rosi had discovered that he lived in Africa and had come to Yugoslavia for the same reasons we had: it was so new to tourism, and he was curious. He'd said he was interested in buying land on the coast because he loved the water and thought it could make a good place for a pied-à-terre in Europe.

"He has a car," said Rosi. "He said he could show us some places. Let's be friendly to him."

I waved at him, and soon we were driving into Dubrovnik and having dinner together. We walked along the town with its stone houses and tiny streets. Dubrovnik was so romantic—

medieval with cobblestoned streets and tiny restaurants with two or three tables outdoors, where they served all kinds of kebabs, with *ajvar,* a red pepper sauce, which I loved.

We sat at one of those outdoor tables, ordered some wine and kebabs, and ate and talked with Pierre for hours. He was older—in his mid-thirties, seventeen years older than I—and had traveled widely. He was so suave, with an enchanting smile. From the moment we sat down at the restaurant, I hung on his every word. He seemed so sophisticated but was very warm and polite. I couldn't believe all the things he had done in his life—an astonishing variety. He had lived in Morocco when he was young, working in a mine and then, when he was eighteen, in a sardine factory. There, he fell in love with a young nurse who was on leave from the Guerre d'Indochine, which Americans called the First Indochina War, so he enlisted in order to follow her there. That seemed incredibly romantic to me, and when I looked in his gray-blue eyes, I held my gaze for a little too long. He smiled.

We sat at that table for a long time, and he kept telling us his stories. The nurse, who was older than Pierre, dropped him, but he couldn't very well unenlist himself; he had to stay on in Vietnam. He was assigned to work in the Sanitation Department, where his duty was to take care of the brothel. When he told us that, Rosi and I exchanged glances, trying hard to keep straight faces. Pierre tilted his head with a little smile and continued. He'd had to sit outside, he said, next to a chart that had a photograph of every woman who worked there. He sat there with a clipboard and ticked off whether she'd had her medical exam, and he counted visits to ensure that all the women were visited equally so that no one was overburdened.

Eventually, Pierre told us, he got typhus. "The only things I could keep down for weeks," he said, "were yogurt and champagne." He clicked glasses with us with our hearty local red wine.

Rosi and I were dazzled.

For the next few days, he took us around the countryside in his car—hiking in the surrounding woods, wandering the local towns. He was a gentleman and full of clever observations and stories. We asked how he ended up working in Africa, which sounded so far away.

He'd been working in the middle of Paris after he came back from Indochina, he told us, in a big, bustling wholesale market called Les Halles, stacking potatoes. He was only doing that for money, until he decided what to do next, and was feeling bored and restless. His sister-in-law had seen an advertisement in the Metro saying they were looking for radio journalists in Africa, and they would send you to school for it if you agreed to stay there for a few years. But she couldn't remember where. So for days, Pierre retraced his sister-in-law's steps, taking the Metro all over Paris, until he finally tracked down the ad. Pierre had a natural voice for radio— very deep, smooth, clear, and authoritative—and a penchant for adventure. It didn't surprise me that he had no trouble getting accepted as a radio journalist.

He'd now been in Africa for ten years. He went first to the

Ivory Coast, he told us, and then to the Central African Republic, in Bangui, where he was now the director of the radio station and minister of information.

I knew I was falling in love. I had never met a man who was so worldly and so kind at once. I liked to think that he was falling in love with me, too.

On one of our evenings, Pierre explained his complicated personal story: He was married, though separated. When he told us, it was as if his face clouded over. He'd fallen in love with a woman of Italian descent who lived in Bangui. They got married, and she started a little boutique of men's clothing with a partner there. "Then she fell in love with him," said Pierre, with a shrug. She'd left him after three years of marriage; they'd now been apart for two years. That's when he started to travel around Europe—to see where he could live, to get out of the Central African Republic, away from his wife and any memories of their time together.

"So that's the story," he said and put down his glass. I felt our joyful mood had changed. I'd been full of hope—maybe a girlish hope, given that he was so much older than I—but I was crushed when I learned he was still married. Even if they'd been separated for two years, even if she was in love with someone else, the fact remained that he was married. Period. The next day, Pierre was his charming self once again, and we were so excited that he seemed happy again we pretended nothing had happened. We went back to having fun exploring Yugoslavia. Before we left to go home, Pierre and I found some time alone. He kissed me and told me I was a charming woman and that he hated to leave me. I didn't want to tear myself away from him, either.

Over the next few weeks, Pierre wrote to me, telling me that he missed me, and finally came to Vienna to visit. We went everywhere together, and I ignored Rosi every time she reminded me that he was married. That didn't matter; I'd decided it was merely a technicality. They were separated; they would get divorced. He was devoted to me.

For the next two years, Pierre courted me, and we kept up a correspondence. Every couple of weeks, one of those tissue-thin airmail letters would arrive with colorful stamps from Africa, and my heart would leap. In each letter, he professed his love for me. "I miss you, I want you next to me," said one. "I can't believe such a young, beautiful, interesting woman is in love with me," said another. "I can't wait to hold you in my arms; I can't stop thinking about you." Each letter was more romantic than the last, and I couldn't wait to see Pierre again.

Between his visits, I went out with other men—dancing, to restaurants, hiking. I told myself that I was young and I wasn't going to stay indoors and wait for a letter. I wanted to have fun. But I did wait for him, in that I saved myself for him. I knew that our relationship was more than just a summer fling. Even though I was young when I met him, and we would certainly have to wait until I was twenty-one to become more serious, there was never any doubt in my mind that Pierre was my great love, my Prince Charming.

· · ·

At some point, perhaps his third visit, it was becoming difficult to see each other because we had no privacy. In those days, you couldn't just go to a hotel if you were unmarried, and you certainly couldn't bring a man home to stay over. We talked and talked and finally decided that we should have a trial period of living together to find out whether we really were compatible—whether this relationship would last. I was very young, but I was convinced that we were a good match. He had more experience, of course, but he loved me; I was certain of that.

We decided that we would rent an apartment for a few weeks before he went back to Africa. It was awkward, because I was the one who had to find somewhere to rent, and I had a lot of doors closed in my face. People assumed I was a prostitute! Finally, we found an apartment in a seedy part of town that I had barely ever visited. It's difficult now to imagine how unconventional it was in those days for an unmarried couple to live together. It simply wasn't done.

When I told Rosi we were going to move in together, she was outraged. A summer flirtation was one thing, but she felt I was destroying not only my reputation but hers and that of our whole family. It would be a stain on my character and hers. How would she ever get married to a decent man if she had a sister who was living in sin? Rosi tried to persuade me not to ruin my life—and her chances.

I knew I was breaking a lot of rules, but I didn't care. I realized it was a daring experiment, but I really didn't think it would give Rosi or my family a bad reputation. My mother and father were shocked, but I refused to change my plan. Ultimately, they let me know that I was responsible for myself. My father, with all of his affairs, could hardly play the morality card with me, and he didn't. I thought that society's morals were a sham anyway. People pretended they were virgins but were sleeping around like bunnies in private. I was actually just being honest, and it was much more important for me to know whether Pierre and I were a good match than to worry about what the neighbors were thinking.

Pierre came back to Vienna, and we went to the dismal apartment, where I lost my virginity. It wasn't the stars and fireworks I expected at first, but I felt much closer to him and glad that we had chosen to try living together. Now I knew I could imagine us being together forever.

When it was time for Pierre to go back to Africa after our three weeks, he asked me to sit down on the ratty sofa in the apartment. He took my face in his hands, and I could see that he wanted to say something serious. I thought this was the moment he was going to propose.

He slowly shook his head before he spoke.

"I don't think it's going to work out," he told me.

I couldn't believe what he'd said. Here I'd staked every-thing—my reputation, my relationship with my sister and my family—on our love. If we didn't get along—if we didn't enjoy making love and didn't make each other laugh—that would be different. But we got along beautifully. He was mouthing words that I couldn't understand. We were going to be married, to be together for life. I was his sweet love, his amour, his light, his life. What about all those love letters he'd written to me? Were they suddenly not true? Was he just toying with me? He'd told me I was beautiful, the perfect woman for him. How could he be telling me it wasn't going to work? That this was adieu?

Pierre kissed me on the forehead, squeezed my hand, and said he was sorry. I gathered my things, and he drove me back to my parents' house. I was in shock. It was the last thing I'd imagined. I endured the drive home in a kind of trance. How could someone who loved you so much just walk out? How could you go from being in love to never seeing each other again?

I'd been so foolish. I wiped away my tears. I wasn't going to allow myself to be brokenhearted.

Mutti wasn't reproachful with me. She knew I was strong and acted as if nothing were wrong. Then she did what only Mutti could do to make the situation better.

"We haven't been to Sistiana for a while," she said. "Let's pack up the Bug and go."

CHAPTER 4

Coming to America

As soon as Mutti and I arrived back home in Vienna, carrying our sandy beach bags up the stairs to our apartment, the housekeeper told us that a foreign man had been calling for me while we were gone. "He phoned every day, sometimes even twice a day," she said. I asked a barrage of questions: Who? What did he say? How did he sound?

"I didn't understand him, because he was speaking a foreign language. I don't know what he wanted," she said, briskly wiping her hands on her apron.

But I knew. I dropped my things in the entryway. It had to have been Pierre, calling to tell me that he still loved me, that he had made a huge mistake and realized that he wanted to be together. He must have changed his mind; otherwise, he wouldn't have called, and certainly not over and over again. I felt as if all were right in the world again; deep down, I'd known it was impossible that he didn't love me. He couldn't have left me after all those love letters, those intimate dinners holding hands across the table, our three weeks living together.

Mutti glanced at me, concerned. She had just spent numerous days consoling me. She thought that after our holiday I'd begun to accept the reality of what had happened and that I'd put this unfortunate affair behind me and moved on. Now she was worried I would get my hopes up, only to be disappointed again. "Let's put our things away, Nori," she said quietly. "Let's get ready for dinner."

But I was too nervous, waiting for the phone to ring again, to do anything but pace around the house. The phone did ring, and to my great relief it was indeed Pierre.

"Nora," he said. "I have to see you. I have to come back to Vienna. I have to talk with your father."

When he said that, I knew he was serious. He was going to ask for my hand in marriage. Tears were streaming down my cheeks, tears of relief and joy.

"Do you still love me?" he asked.

"Oui," I replied.

Just two days later, I was in his arms again. When I picked him up at the airport, he hugged me tightly and didn't let go for a long time. "I'm never going to leave you again," he said, stroking my cheek with a finger. We went to a café, where he explained that he'd had to leave because his wife had asked him to come to London, to try one last time to see if they could be together.

I felt immensely relieved; I had been so baffled by the way he'd left. It was not that he didn't love me; it was because he was being loyal and decent to his wife. He felt he owed it to her to try once more.

"I felt I owed her that," he said, reiterating all of this. He looked down at his coffee, stirring. In a low voice, he told me the story: His wife had apologized and told him she'd made a big mistake when she'd left him. The man she'd left him for turned out to be quite different from what she'd thought, and they'd split up. She regretted everything.

"But I couldn't go back," Pierre said, looking me in the eyes. "I was no longer in love with her." He squeezed my hand. "All I could think about was you."

I wasn't angry with him or even wary. At the time, perhaps naive in my youth, I felt strongly that I was the most important thing in his life, and he knew he had made a mistake. He had needed to find me. I understood that he'd needed to go to London: they had been married for several years, and he couldn't split up with her without meeting one last time, to know for sure that their relationship was over. He had to find out the truth about how he was feeling. If our relationship could stand that test, then it was real. If he hadn't gone back to see her, to realize that their relationship was dead and he was in love with me, it would have lingered in the back of his mind and cast a shadow over our love affair. Now he was free from his emotional tie to his wife. I never thought that he didn't love me, but the fact that he went back to his wife to be sure it was over was proof that he was finished with her and eager to start a new life—with me.

"I never meant to hurt you," he said. "But I didn't want to hurt her, either. I wanted everything to be clean and clear. If I knew for sure that we were finished, I had to be able to say that to her face." I trusted Pierre; he had done what he thought was the right thing for everyone. "I was so afraid that you wouldn't take me back," he said. I reached up, stroked his hair, and said, "I knew you would come back." He leaned across the table and kissed my hands.

"I want to marry you," he said.

My mother was worried. But she was also happy for me— she knew how much I loved him, how much I wanted to be with him—and she could see that we loved each other. She was sad to see me leaving.

But I loved what Pierre represented: he was a man who had traveled, who had adventures, who was willing to start a new life with me in a foreign country; it was the tone I wanted my life to have. Of course, things didn't turn out exactly as I had expected.

Pierre and I made plans to get married as soon as we could. We talked about our future, and he reminded me that he had no prospects for a job in Europe; he was working in Africa. He knew I wouldn't be keen about moving to Africa, so he'd found another job, working as a radio journalist for the Voice of America in the United States. He asked me where I wanted to live—in Africa or the United States?

He laid out the options. In Africa, he told me, I would live like a queen. He would have the job of minister of information in Burundi, and we would have a large house with servants. "Life will be easy," he said. If we went to Africa, his career would take a step forward. He also had a guaranteed job as a news director. In America, on the other hand, his career would take two steps backward. He would be only a radio host, and given that he wasn't an American citizen, his prospects for advancing were nil. He wouldn't make much money, and it might be difficult.

I knew he would gladly go back to his comfortable life in Africa, but he insisted the decision was up to me. As much as I loved to travel, I wasn't interested in going to Africa, to live among expatriates. There, I knew, I would have an easy life of lying in the sun drinking gin and tonics with nothing to do. That's not the kind of person I am; I like to be active and involved; like my mother, I didn't picture myself as a housewife. Also, Pierre had lived in Africa already for ten years, with his wife and their friends, and I thought it was important for us to have a fresh start. Not that I wasn't nervous about moving to the United States—I'd heard scary things about America, that people carried guns, that they only ate fast food and drove everywhere on six-lane highways—but in the end I decided I preferred it to Africa.

"America," I said.

"All right," he said. "America."

Pierre wanted to formally ask my father for my hand in marriage. I liked that he honored that tradition, because I knew it would please my father to be shown such respect. Not that my father was easily convinced. Both he and my mother were concerned that Pierre was not an appropriate match for me: he was so much older, a foreigner, and still not divorced, and he currently had no promise of financial security. Most important, he was taking me away from my family to a foreign country. Other than the fact that Pierre was utterly charming, it would have been difficult for my parents to imagine a worse match for me. My father agreed to speak with him if we could have a neutral translator, so we decided to meet Pierre with my sister Rosi.

Rosi could translate, but she was hardly neutral. She had been comfortable when Pierre and I flirted on the beach, but marrying him was another story. As far as she was concerned, I was completely crazy, throwing my life away.

"He's closer to Mutti's age than your age!" she said.

"I don't care," I told her. "If we have ten great years together, that's more than most couples."

We were to meet at the Cobenzl, a famous restaurant high above Vienna with a sweeping view of the Danube and the city. That morning, I drove to the hairdresser to pick up my mother. She sat quietly next to me, then squeezed my hand.

"You will be so far away," she said and dabbed at her eyes. I had rarely seen her cry.

Rosi and I took a long time to get dressed. I wore a simple A-line dress in pastel blue. Rosi put on her tailored summer suit. We both wore our pearls and pumps with low heels. Mutti had on her second-best dark blue dress with a matching jacket and her best pearls. Vati wore a suit with his usual light gray Spencer Tracy hat.

We drove together to the Cobenzl, an old hunting castle with a formal restaurant and garden, which my parents had chosen so that we might be able to have a private conversation. The weather was perfect—it was late summer—and we sat among the flowers and trees in comfortable chairs. Waiters in black uniforms appeared and disappeared like magic.

When Pierre arrived, looking dashing in his summer blazer, with no hat—he had beautiful curls—he and my parents exchanged stiff handshake greetings. Pierre gave them his big smile.

My mother wasn't her usual upbeat self. She knew that if I married Pierre, I would leave Austria, and she would hardly see me, her baby. Christa was already off and married, and Rosi had plans to go to Paris, so she would be left alone. I could no longer pick up and travel with her to Italy, and even visiting would have to be restricted to once or perhaps twice a year because I would be so far away. She barely touched her lunch.

Pierre ordered veal kidneys for lunch, which, to my parents, only further emphasized his foreignness, because Austrians aren't anywhere near as enthusiastic about offal as the French are. I noticed my father glanced at my mother when the waiter took the order. From the moment the meal began, my father was much more businesslike, grilling Pierre as if he were at a job interview. Without wasting any time on small talk, my father asked Pierre how he would support me. He also asked for the details about Pierre's divorce proceedings. He insisted that we have a prenuptial agreement and a contract stipulating that I was a free person and not dependent on him.

"The French law does not give women much freedom," my father said, sipping a glass of white wine. "They treat women like maids." He insisted that I keep my Austrian citizenship. Pierre readily agreed to all of my father's wishes.

Eventually, my father turned to me and asked what I wanted. I had been nervous throughout lunch but didn't think my father would refuse Pierre. Underneath his brusqueness, it was clear that he and my mother were beginning to warm to Pierre as a person. You could practically see my mother thaw under Pierre's smile and gentlemanly manners.

"Do you understand what you're doing?" my father asked me. "You're leaving your family and your country to go with someone new, nearly a stranger, to a strange country." I bristled at having my Pierre described as a stranger—I felt that I was an adult, I knew what I was doing, and I loved him—but I also felt a twinge of guilt that I would be leaving my parents. Still, I wanted to live my own life, and my parents were the very ones who had instilled that value in me. I nodded and glanced at Pierre, who smiled warmly back at me. I was certain.

"This is what you want?" my father asked again.

"Yes," I said. "I'm sure."

Pierre then formally asked my father if he could marry me.

"Well," said my father, glancing at my mother, who nodded. "Yes." Pierre and my father stood up, shook hands, and then embraced me. My mother opened her arms and hugged Pierre, too. She was upset, but she approved; she liked him. My parents were torn; they didn't want me to leave, but they could see that I was truly in love. Pierre had won them over with his warmth and honesty, and they would not get in the way of our happiness. They trusted him with me.

We wanted to get married quickly, because Pierre's job in Washington, D.C., was waiting, but there were formalities we had to attend to. We were going to have a traditional Catholic wedding ceremony in a church, to please my grandmother, and then be officially married at the French embassy in Vienna, where we also had to post the banns some weeks in advance.

In the meantime, we drove from Austria to France so that I could meet Pierre's family. On the way, Pierre wanted to stop for lunch at a *routier*, a simple, unassuming restaurant by the highway where truck drivers stop; in France, the truck drivers are discerning about what they eat, so the *routiers* are known for great food.

Because of my education at Vienna's French school, I was not surprised when the lunch came in multiple small courses, which was still unlike the way we ate in Austria. Then, for dessert, a *plat de fromage* arrived, a cheese platter with probably six different cheeses. I had never seen so many cheeses in my life! I loved it and immediately cut the point off the brie and big chunks off all the other cheeses to put on my plate. When I cut the brie, you could hear a gasp throughout the dining room.

Pierre thought it was funny, even when the waiter rushed over and complained, "Monsieur, monsieur!" As I quickly learned, no one cuts the tip off the brie—it is considered the height of rudeness—because the brie ripens from the middle, which is the best part; it's like going straight for the artichoke heart. The French take delicate slices—lengthwise—to finish off their wine with some bread. I had no idea, because in Austria we mostly eat hard cheeses and certainly not at the end of the meal. I was mortified when I realized that the whole dining room was staring at me. I felt like a total foreigner.

Pierre was amused at my innocent mistake and appeased the waiter, promising to pay double for the cheese. He held my hand and told me not to worry, and so, as the other diners turned away, I enjoyed every bite of my brie.

I was excited to visit Paris for the first time. From the moment we arrived, I was awed by its scale. Everything seemed so grand. Vienna is a formal city with beautiful architecture, but Paris seemed so much more impressive, with its wide boulevards, enormous public plazas, graceful arcades, and buildings with ornate balconies.

Pierre drove us straight to the center of the city, to a typical three-story apartment building, where his favorite niece, Nathalie, lived; she was just a little older than I was. We entered through a tall gate and courtyard and climbed the stairs to the apartment, which had high ceilings, a tiny kitchen, and a bathroom where you had to step over the toilet to get to the shower. The place was cozy and decorated in an eclectic style, with a few antiques and some modern pieces.

Nathalie was a bit reserved; I think she was taken aback that I was so young. After all, I was seventeen years younger than Pierre, and nearly thirty years younger than his older sister. Pierre already had six grandnephews and grandnieces! Nathalie was very Parisian—she spoke so quickly I could barely understand her—and dressed conservatively in a knee-length skirt and twinset. She was kind to me, though, explaining to me details about all the members of the family and where they lived in Paris.

Later, I met the rest of Pierre's family. We had lunch with his two sisters at his brother Jean's apartment in the 6th arrondissement in St.-Germain-des-Prés. That apartment, too, was on a grand scale, filled with light from lots of windows, as well as Persian rugs, paintings, and Art Nouveau furniture. It even had a maid's quarters. I was a bit intimidated, particularly because his family was so intellectual. Pierre's brother Jean was an ethnoanthropologist and friends with many philosophers and writers. His wife, Den, sizzled with intelligence. As it turned out, Pierre's siblings were very welcoming. I imagined they might be unfriendly, as Parisians were reputed to be, and critical of the fact that I was so much younger and a foreigner. Instead, they greeted me warmly, praised my French, and told me how pleased they were that their little brother had finally found someone he was so happy with. They had never met his wife in Africa, and so they were glad to meet me and feel more included in his life. They could also see that we were very much in love.

We had a wonderful time in Paris—how can you not have a great time in Paris? We made the rounds of intimate dinners with each of Pierre's siblings, as well as his friends, meeting their children. We walked all over the city, peeking into shopwindows, courtyards, and churches. At the time, Pierre had money to burn because he'd worked in Africa for so long with so little to buy, so he took me out to great restaurants. Every meal was an experience, opening up new worlds of wine, sauces, and tastes to me. My favorite was Androuet, famous for its elaborate cheese platters. The cheese, of course, normally comes at the end of the meal. But I decided I wanted nothing else. "I am saving myself for the cheese," I told Pierre, who warned me that this was a bad idea and more sensibly ordered veal scallops and a green salad. I conceded a little and joined him with a small salad but held out for the cheese course. When ten trays of cheese arrived, each one laden with ten different types of cheese, I couldn't contain myself. Even though I only took little slices, it was as if I had eaten two pounds of butter. I came home, and my whole system went into shock from the fat. I was ill all night. It was the last time I ever ate that much cheese. That was when I learned that Pierre knew what he was talking about when it came to French food.

Pierre had also introduced me to the pleasures of French red wine, which I still adore. He chose mostly Burgundies. In Austria, we usually drank white wine, and though I'd had red wine with Aki, French reds were unlike any I'd ever tasted before. To have wine with every meal, and different wines every time, felt like the height of civilization! At the end of the meal, I'd end up a little tipsy, the world shiny around me; it was the best sort of vacation I could have imagined. Not once did I think about the future or what I had to do; I was simply being taken care of and introduced to an entirely new world by my fiancé. It was wonderful.

Before we left, Pierre took me shopping so I'd have some new clothes to take to America. He went to his tailor for new suits and shirts, and then we stopped at Yves Saint Laurent, where I bought buttery suede pants with a matching belt and a dark brown cashmere sweater. In another store, he bought me a white fur coat, nutria with a mink collar. I felt so stylish, ready to take on America.

When we returned to Vienna, we planned to be married right away. Because the Catholic Church didn't recognize Pierre's first marriage—it hadn't taken place in a church—he was, according to it, single, and so we could have a church wedding immediately. After our wedding, we would go on our honeymoon while we waited for his official divorce papers to come through, after which we'd get legally married at the French embassy. The wedding was all arranged very quickly. After the priest agreed to marry us, we had to take a week of instruction with him before he would perform the ceremony. We had two weeks to prepare. I had a beautiful white lace dress made, with long sleeves and a tight bodice, along with a little veil. We invited just family and a few friends, perhaps fifteen people in all.

The wedding took place on a warm, clear, late summer day—September 19, 1965. I was twenty-one. We got married near my family's house, in St. Jakob's Chapel at the end of the Eroicagasse, a tiny twelfth-century stone chapel with simple wooden benches and an altar. I'd never dreamed about a fancy wedding; I preferred a simple ceremony with my family.

I was a little nervous at the wedding; it suddenly dawned on me that this was serious! Now I was supposed to be with this man and leave my family. It was a very emotional day for everyone, both joyous and bittersweet. I knew I would see them all again—people do travel, though they did not travel at the time as they do today—but I also knew it would never be the same. Still, as I stood next to Pierre, saying the vows, I had no doubts.

We had chosen Prague for our honeymoon because it was one of the few cities in Europe that had escaped bombing during the war. On top of that, in 1965 Czechoslovakia had just opened its borders to foreigners for travel, and we loved the idea of being among the first to visit. Prague looked like a city out of a fairy tale, with its peaked red roofs, the Charles Bridge over the Vltava River, and fifteenth-century castles. The city was an architectural wonder, intact from medieval times with beautiful baroque touches but very gray and dirty, from the coal that was burned for heat.

We were eager to explore but first had to find a place to stay, which was not easy in those days, because it was under Communist rule and had only recently opened to tourism; had no hotels or inns for travelers. So we went to the government tourist office, where a dour-faced official offered us only a room in a private home, located quite far outside the old center of town. People would give up their bedrooms and sleep in the living room to make a little extra money, he explained, and we would all share the house. Our faces fell. Because I spoke German, I was able to make the government officer understand that it was our honeymoon, and we wanted to stay in a hotel. He finally relented and gave us permission to stay at Prague's only hotel that accepted foreigners, built for businessmen and airline employees. We thought we had scored a victory until we saw our room: it was spare and drab, with only two tiny twin beds.

We were both astonished. I was exhausted, and this was not at all how I'd pictured my honeymoon! I was ready to cry. Then Pierre sat down on the bed, took me onto his lap, and began to laugh. I couldn't help but laugh with him, and I understood then that whatever happened in our marriage, if we had the capacity to laugh about it, we would be okay. I was relieved that Pierre didn't scream at anyone in the hotel or make a scene; he just curled his six-foot-three frame onto the bed and cuddled me closer, and eventually we went to sleep.

Over the next few days, we walked around Prague, exploring the Prague Castle and the beautiful parks. There were, however, very few places for tourists to eat. We finally walked into a simple place inside a dark stone house, with trestle tables. We looked at the menu but couldn't figure it out at all. Fortunately, the waiter understood a bit of German. First, he brought us mugfuls of cold, flavorful amber beer. We drank that with smoked fish and a stew. For dessert, he brought a big pile of very strong gorgonzola cheese riced together with good butter, which we ate with sourdough bread. We wrote down the name of the cheese dish from the menu and ordered it everywhere else we went, and enjoyed it for the rest of the trip. We had such fun visiting a new culture and country together, which seemed like an auspicious prelude to our adventure in America.

Finally, Pierre's divorce papers came through, and we were officially married at the French embassy on December 3, 1965. We left for America shortly thereafter. I packed with a careful eye, wanting to look elegant in my new country. I also wanted to make a good impression on Pierre's boss, who had arranged to pick us up from the airport, so I dressed up for the journey in a nice suit with gloves, with my hair and makeup carefully done. I was nervous about flying, but Pierre reassured me; he'd flown back and forth from Africa many times. The plane across the Atlantic seemed as if it took forever, and from New

York we had to take yet another plane—a small propeller plane this time—to Washington, D.C.

When we finally arrived, late at night, Pierre's boss took us first to the only hotel close to his office that would accept the dog Pierre had brought along from Africa, a small griffon named Ourson. The hotel, which was near Union Station, was named the Dodge House—a name that is nearly impossible to pronounce if you speak French or German. We had a difficult time making ourselves understood to taxi drivers those first few days.

I was excited to be in Washington because, at least on a map, it appeared to be a bit like Vienna: It had the Potomac River flowing through it and lots of green spaces and trees, like the Danube and the Vienna Woods. It had older buildings, museums downtown, and the majestic Capitol. I thought the city was beautiful, but I was disappointed in the Potomac. When I went to its banks, I saw signs saying that the water was polluted and that you must not swim in it. I had envisioned bathing in it as you do in the Danube, but that, of course, was out of the question.

Our first night in the hotel was difficult. Ourson was dehydrated and sick from the flight, and as soon as we went to sleep, I was awakened by sirens. I froze in fright: I immediately thought of the sirens that sounded before a bomb went off in Vienna when I was a child, and it took a while to get used to feeling that we were safe. It was the strangest flashback.

There were a lot of other little things to get used to. We took Ourson everywhere with us, as one does with a small dog in Europe, and people were outraged. "How dare you bring a dog in here?" they would demand in shops. We would also try to find a place to eat that served dinner later; we couldn't get used to the American custom of eating at six in the evening. The first evening we tried the hotel restaurant and had no idea what the waitress was saying when she offered a "buff-it," instead of a buffet, which we pronounce "boo-fay" in French. Finally, we decided we would eat at Union Station, because we could tie the dog up outside the restaurant and it was open late.

It was nearly Christmas when we arrived in Washington, and we knew very few people. But Pierre had a few American friends who had worked in the State Department in the Central African Republic with him. One couple, Bob and Domnica, invited us to spend Christmas dinner with them. It was a lovely invitation; it would have been so depressing to spend Christmas alone in our little hotel. We could also bring Ourson, who still hadn't quite recovered from his trip to the United States.

"Ourson looks terrible," Domnica said, "like a little rag!"

"What should we do for him?" asked Pierre.

"Make him a big bowl of rice and some ground meat," Domnica said and proceeded to do just that. It perked Ourson back up, and after that he ate nothing else.

As we began to settle in, it quickly emerged that I would be responsible for setting up our new lives. This surprised me. I hadn't expected to have to figure out where we were going to live and shop; having married an older man, I thought he was going to take care of me, as he had done in Paris. It was quite an awakening to realize, at twenty-two, that it was going to be up to me to find a house, turn it into a home, create a social life, learn to shop and cook and do laundry. On the one hand, I was disillusioned; until then, I'd thought of Pierre as my Prince Charming. On the other, it forced me to become an independent person, to be productive, to meet people, to cultivate a circle of friends, to find the right food shops, to figure out how to budget his small income, and to learn a lot of the skills that would serve me later in life. It was these skills that I continued to fall back on—especially knowing how to budget properly to run a restaurant!

Dressed in my white fur coat and hat, I met with a real estate agent and went all over Georgetown and surrounding areas searching for a dog-friendly apartment within our budget. The fact that Pierre was only making $10,000 a year at his new job meant that we could barely afford about $250 a month in rent, and I quickly realized that making do on his new salary was not going to be as romantic as I thought. Still, I eventually found a small wooden house in Tenleytown with a tiny kitchen and a garden. It was a charming bungalow, with a front porch, which was unlike anything I'd seen in Europe, as well as a porch in the back. The yard was perfect for a dog and had a grill with a rotisserie attachment, where, it turned out, we would cook most of our meals. The kitchen was tiny, with very old appliances, but I didn't care. I fell in love with a painting on the wall, which looked like a Toulouse-Lautrec bar scene and reminded me of Paris, which made me feel at home. The place was owned by a Frenchwoman, who took pity on us and rented it for a decent price. It was a long commute for Pierre but otherwise a cozy house in a friendly neighborhood.

The day we moved in, I opened the freezer, then slammed it shut. Inside was a package that I read as "COBRA." I quickly called Shelley Getchell, whom Pierre had known in Africa and one of the few people I knew in Washington.

"Do they really eat snake in America?" I asked, trying to sound nonchalant.

"Read me the package," she said, laughing.

I spelled out "O-K-R-A." My English skills, combined with my nervousness about settling in, had led to some confusion! But to this day, I can't eat okra without thinking about snake.

Shelley's husband was a Foreign Service officer who worked with the U.S. Information Agency and had helped Pierre get his Voice of America job. Shelley was a kind, good-looking woman, tall and elegant, with a New England patrician air. She would patiently speak English with me, which helped me become more fluent. Before Pierre and I got a car, she would pick me up and bring me to her house to do laundry and take me shopping.

I was overwhelmed by American supermarkets, which I found very large. The parking lot seemed like a city block. And the carts! Who would need to buy so much food that they had to put it in a trolley? In Europe, of course, you go from store to store every day with your basket or bag—to the butcher, the charcuterie, the dairy shop, the baker, the greengrocer, the cheese store. Here, everything was under one roof, and it all looked so sterile. All the food was packaged and had no smell.

But Shelley would commandeer a cart and steer it around that huge place, chatting the whole time. "First we go on the outside, where the produce is," she said. The produce section was very small; there was only iceberg lettuce and broccoli and mostly oranges or apples or very hard green pears. A few pale cucumbers and tomatoes. No herbs. No fresh greens. Nothing that was remotely recognizable to me.

Shelley saw my face fall. "No," she said, "you won't find fresh garlic or parsley here, and not much variety."

The dairy section was another disappointment.

"We're not in France," said Shelley with a smile. The only cheeses I could find that seemed like something we would want to eat were a strong cheddar and something smelly like limburger; everything else came in sheets wrapped in plastic and looked like plastic itself. But what horrified me most were the breads. There were rows and rows of Wonder bread or a similar type, which had no smell and was so squishy you could take an entire loaf and form it into a wet little ball. The "gourmet" bread hardly looked any different. There was such a vast quantity of food and hardly anything I recognized or wanted to buy or eat.

Shelley continued wheeling. "Here's the meat section," she said, parking in front of a deli case filled with packaged meat.

"Where is the butcher?" I asked. How could you cook meat without asking about the quality and the cut? Shelley just shook her head. "No butcher." She explained that you could ring a bell and ask for a package of meat to be cut into smaller portions, but that was it.

Shelley continued to add packages to her cart until it was nearly full.

"Shelley," I said, shocked. "We're not buying for the whole week!"

"We are," she said. "That's how we do it in this country." I didn't understand; by the end of the week, none of those vegetables, which looked sorry to begin with, would even be edible. But I didn't say anything. I was in a new country and trying to fit in.

As we checked out, perhaps what surprised me most was how impersonal the supermarket was. In Europe, shopping is a very social event. You go to the butcher and talk about what you're planning to make and how many people will need to be fed. He recommends a cut and perhaps a recipe, and you ask about his wife and whether her back is feeling any better: you have a conversation. It's the same with the baker; he greets you with "The usual, ma'am?" and tells you what's fresh from the oven. The greengrocer lets you know that he just got the first raspberries in or the first asparagus. There was a lot of community feeling and personal interaction shopping in Europe. But at the American supermarket, they barely grunted at you when you took the things out of your shopping cart and cashed out. You could get out of there without ever speaking to anyone at all, which seemed very sad and lonely to me. At least Shelley had turned it into a game, guiding me through that maze of packaged, frozen, and artificial foods I had never seen before.

Eventually, I began to branch out to find foods that were more familiar to me. Shelley introduced me to the French market, where, while I couldn't afford the meat or many of the other ingredients, I was happy to find lovely baguettes. At the Italian market, I found olive oil, Italian cheeses, olives, and pesto. I had only fifty dollars a week to spend on food, so I had to budget it wisely. We ended up eating a lot of chuck steak—we loved to grill outside, because barbecuing was a novelty to us Europeans—along with salad and French bread, washed down with red California wine that came in a jug. I suppose it isn't surprising that I lost two dress sizes my first year in the United States. Partly it was because Pierre never ate between meals and didn't like sweets. But also, I couldn't find the pastries, charcuterie, fresh dark bread, and butter that would have tempted me as they had in Vienna. I had yet to be exposed to what was delicious about regional American cuisine; that would come later.

After shopping, Shelley would bring me over to her house so I could do laundry, because we had no washer or dryer at home yet. I had never even seen a dryer, and at home in Austria we had no washing machine; my mother rented one every two weeks and took care of our laundry that way, hanging it out to dry. While I waited for my clothes to get clean, we would make ourselves lunch. Shelley introduced me to the art of the sandwich. We became queens of the refrigerator clean out, putting whatever leftovers we found into salads or sandwiches.

Sometimes we'd open a can of soup and spike it with fresh herbs or more vegetables. We ate these lunches with a glass of red wine and always enjoyed ourselves. I loved that feeling of being creative in the kitchen, with a friend, even if we were just making sandwiches or doctoring up soup.

One afternoon, Shelley had errands to run while my laundry was finishing, so I stayed back and entertained myself by browsing her bookshelf. I pulled out a book called *French Provincial Cooking* by Elizabeth David. I lay back on the sofa and began paging through it, and soon I was completely immersed. I felt for the first time that I was reading a book by someone who was writing exactly the way I thought about food but had never been able to articulate myself. The author didn't give you recipes by the cup or the teaspoon; she gave you the whole feeling of the dish and the place by describing it vividly. She made me understand that the most important thing was the ingredients—they should be fresh, seasonal, and natural—and that the best way to prepare them is very simply, letting the flavors speak for themselves.

As my clothes were spinning in the dryer, I went on a journey with Elizabeth David through the provinces of France. We started in Provence, where I was mesmerized by the perfect summer picnic: a table laid with black olives, some ripe tomatoes, "a pyramid of little green figs baked by the sun," followed by a *pissaladière*—an onion and anchovy tart—tender little artichokes in oil, and a roast of lamb cooked on the spit. In Paris, she described beautifully prepared vegetables, like gratins or purees, and "soups delicately colored like summer dresses, coral, ivory or pale green." In Normandy, she talked about the charcuterie—terrines and gelatins, pâtés and galantines, all made of duck. Outside, the vegetable stalls are "piled high with Breton artichokes, perfectly round with tightly closed leaves; long, clean shining leeks; and fluffy green-white cauliflowers." I closed my eyes, picturing this bounty, and then imagined the produce section at my neighborhood grocery store—what a contrast!

I kept reading long after my clothes had dried and Shelley returned home. "What are you reading?" she asked. "Just a minute," I replied, abstractedly. I was too absorbed to even stop to talk. I felt as if I were under a spell. David explained how important it was to pay attention to the details, such as the order in which you put the ingredients in a pot so that they would come out perfectly cooked at the same time. Everything she described as a recipe told a story about a place, right down to the seasons and the earth.

But what impressed me most weren't the sauces and cooking techniques, or the complicated French dishes, but the way she described the simplest of meals. One was the omelet served at the Poulard Hotel at Mont St.-Michel, which was so light, fluffy, and flavorful that many people tried to understand its secret. Finally, Madame Poulard wrote the recipe in 1922, nine years before her death: "I break some good eggs in a bowl, I beat them well, I put a good piece of butter in the pan, I throw the eggs into it, and I shake it constantly." That was it.

David's description of the perfect omelet, a "soft bright golden roll plump and spilling out a little at the edges," not a "busy, important urban dish but something gentle and pastoral, with the clean scent of the dairy, the kitchen garden, the basket of early morning mushrooms or the sharp tang of freshly picked herbs," was a revelation to me. It was all about the ingredients—the good eggs and butter, the freshly picked herbs. Whatever the recipe, I realized, what mattered most was what went into it.

I closed the book, longing to be in Europe, feasting on one of those delicious omelets. It was the first time I truly understood how important it was to find fresh, local, wholesome ingredients. Perhaps I had to be in the United States, or at least my experience of it thus far, with acres of frozen and packaged foods, to have something that might seem so obvious to a European hit me in the face like that.

Reading Elizabeth David's book made me hungry—not just for the tight, round artichokes and firm cauliflowers piled in tidy little rows in the country markets, or fresh-baked, crusty bread, or homemade charcuterie, or cheeses from Camembert to Livarot. I was hungry to go find fresh, beautiful foods for myself—ingredients that speak for themselves.

I thought I would start by finding a farmer who sold freshly laid eggs or a baker who made his own daily bread. I was young and optimistic and was sure I could find those foods. I didn't know how; I just knew it depended on me.

CHAPTER 5

Dinner Parties

One morning, over coffee, Pierre casually mentioned to me that we ought to have a few friends over for dinner. "We've been invited out so much," he said. "We need to return the favor."

He was right: Within a few months of being in Washington, I'd begun to make friends—people from Pierre's workplace and friends of theirs from the State Department or the French embassy—and many of them had invited us over for meals. It seemed that almost every night we went to someone's house for a dinner party and an evening of playing bridge and drinking wine. I would often arrive early and park myself in the kitchen so I could watch our friends cook, and help, of course. Most of them were marvelous cooks, making international specialties in their tiny Washington, D.C., kitchens, transporting us to their home countries—Morocco, Cameroon, Belgium, and of course France.

With all these great cooks inviting us to dinner, I was apprehensive about having them over to our house. I was not yet very accomplished in the kitchen, as many of them were, and had no experience entertaining. They seemed to effortlessly take things from the stove to the table with exact timing, never missing a bon mot in a witty conversation. But I was inexperienced and nervous. Still, when Pierre asked me to invite a couple of friends over to dinner, I had to agree.

By this time, I had devoured Elizabeth David's books and must have tried nearly every one of her recipes—at least the ones for which I could find the ingredients. I had realized that cooking was not just about throwing something in the pan and hoping for the best. It involved basic cooking techniques and understanding the ingredients you start with, which had to be absolutely fresh and flavorful. I began to experiment, learning knife skills first and practicing slicing and chopping, even deboning chickens, ducks, and turkeys. I wanted to make delicious dishes my husband and our friends would enjoy.

I began planning the dinner party. I knew I could get a fresh chicken from Virginia, so I decided to make Elizabeth David's famous roast chicken. The recipe called for seasoning the chicken and roasting it for twenty minutes on one side, twenty minutes on the other, then turning it breast side up to cook for an additional twenty minutes so that it would be browned and crispy, not dried out. I decided to serve David's *oeufs en cocotte* as an appetizer. I went out and bought special ramekins for the recipe—an indulgence for us at the time. The recipe involved putting a raw egg in a buttered ramekin, covering it with cream, grated nutmeg, and a bit of salt and pepper, then covering it all with aluminum foil and cooking it for five to eight minutes in a water bath in a preheated oven. We would follow with a roasted chicken. We would finish with a green salad, tossed with a simple vinaigrette, along with some garlic and herbs. Dessert was several cheeses—a brie from the French market and a decent cheddar from the supermarket deli case. We'd finish with coffee and a bit of chocolate. Of course, we'd drink red wine throughout dinner; I'd often buy the Mountain Red from Almaden or Gallo in large half-gallon jugs, which I poured into a nice glass decanter that Pierre had brought from France. We also had his Christofle silverware, which made things feel a little more special and elegant. As I conceived of it, the meal seemed foolproof.

I cleaned the house, prepared the food and table, and waited nervously for our friends to arrive. I served them all some vodka gimlets to start. We settled in to some conversation. Everyone spoke French; Pierre and I were improving our English by watching Walter Cronkite and Alfred Hitchcock movies. About an hour later, our friend from the Belgian embassy, Alain Rens, turned to me. "Nora, we're half-drunk, and still there's no food. What are you cooking? Do you need help?"

I waved away his offer and went into the kitchen, but he followed me anyway. He opened the oven, then peered at the temperature gauge and scowled. Then he laughed. "Fahrenheit, Nora," he said. "Not centigrade!"

The chicken was still nearly raw.

Alain thought it was funny, but I was mortified. Until now, I'd mainly been using the outside grill, not the oven. Here I'd planned for a perfect evening and wanted to impress everybody. It had been so important to Pierre that we give our friends a lovely meal.

But I didn't have many options, so I opened a bottle of wine and turned up the oven. "We'll start with the appetizer," I told Alain, as thankfully, they were ready. He helped me carry the ramekins to the table.

After I set down the dishes, one of our other guests looked at his with dismay. "I'm sorry, I can't eat that egg, and especially not with cream," he said.

What had I done now? How had I ruined it?

"I have high cholesterol," he said, pushing it away, apologetically.

I was shocked. I had never heard of anyone who couldn't eat something for health reasons, so here was another learning experience. I had always regarded foods as healing, but here I was discovering that for some people it's the opposite.

At home in Austria, cream—or *Schlag,* as it is called in Vienna—is like a national food. You have coffee with *Schlag,* apple strudel with *Schlag;* even my father, who ate so healthfully, loved to eat canned pineapple with a big spoonful of *Schlag.* My mother always had cream on hand. And eggs! They are the base of so many foods. I was flabbergasted. It seemed like a punishment not to be able to eat *oeufs en cocotte,* scrambled eggs, hard-boiled eggs for an afternoon snack, or noodles mixed with eggs and ham and baked into a casserole. Eggs were the most primary of foods; this was, for me, astonishing, to think that someone could be deprived of these most primary food categories. I had never thought that these basic foods could be bad for somebody. It made me begin to think differently about what it meant to eat healthfully, even at this early point.

Alain, once again, came to my rescue. "I'll have two!" he said gleefully and complimented the eggs.

We opened more wine, and eventually—perhaps a good half hour later—the chicken was done, and it was delicious. It was very simple: I just rubbed the skin with olive oil, salt, and pepper and stuffed the cavity with lemon, an onion, and some tarragon, just as Elizabeth David suggested. Everyone ate his or her fill, and finally I was able to relax. I met more and more friends who were good cooks. Pierre worked with Georges Collinet, who was half-Cameroonian and half-French and had a Voice of America radio show that introduced American music to an African audience and vice versa. The first time I met Georges, he invited us to dinner at his Georgetown apartment, which was in the basement. But Georges insisted Georgetown was the only place to live in D.C., which is why he put up with his dark flat. But his small living quarters didn't stop him from holding big dinner parties. Everything about Georges was big—his size, his personality, his love of life, his smile.

Georges and I became fast friends. He always had splendid dinner parties. That first evening, I complimented him on his food and asked him a lot of questions about it, and he told me that next time I should come early and help him cook.

From then on, Georges and I would make complicated dishes together—pâtés, roasts. Once we deboned a duck and stuffed a chicken inside. No matter what we were eating, he always had good French red wine on hand to accompany the dish. Each time I visited, it seemed he had a different girlfriend, but our friendship remained a constant. The only problem with Georges was that if you went to his house for dinner at 8:00, you never sat down to the table until 10:30. He didn't even step into the kitchen with the grocery bags until 8:00.

"Georges," I inevitably told him. "When someone is invited to your house for dinner, they have to have eaten before coming to survive." But he just gave me that broad smile of his and poured me another glass of wine.

Another new friend who had a great influence on my cooking was Nicole Macaire, whose husband worked at the French embassy. We met on a harbor cruise in Baltimore that the State Department had organized for new employees from other countries. Nicole was tiny and birdlike, like so many Frenchwomen, and, when we met, very pregnant with her fourth child. We spoke French together, and she invited me over for dinner soon after.

What really impressed me about Nicole was that she had a small budget, especially with all the children, but managed, through her creativity, to turn out sophisticated meals and throw memorable parties. She turned her basement into a sort of bar and lounge, with a warm, moody atmosphere, where we would dance after dinner. She showed me some tricks for making great food inexpensively. One trick in particular that I recall is how she made beef tartare. She bought cheap hamburger meat and then kneaded it with ice-cold hands so that the fat stuck to her skin. She then removed the fat by washing her hands repeatedly, and when she was finished, the meat was lean and flavorful. Then she mixed in spices, herbs, capers, mustard, and egg yolks, and it tasted like the best tartare in France. She gave me confidence that it was possible to cook well, and to make great-tasting food, even on a small budget. And she involved me; she asked me to bring things along. She made it look effortless; somehow, even with four kids and a working husband, she made it all come together calmly. She was very French in this way, and I learned a lot from her.

It seemed all of our friends had their own international specialties. Muriel Maufroy, who worked with Pierre, liked to cook Asian food, which was popular at the time. It was at her home that I first tasted Asian-inspired dishes, such as poached salmon with Vietnamese cellophane noodle salad, using ingredients such as soy and ginger that I had never been exposed to before. Another friend, Nina Sutton, who was half-French with a North African father, introduced me to North African cuisine, such as *tagines* and couscous. Alain and his wife, Danielle, had access to ingredients from the Belgian and French embassies—wines, cheeses, even Belgian endives. Danielle didn't cook, but Alain, like Georges, was very accomplished in the kitchen, which was unusual to me—all these men cooking. Every dinner party seemed like a culinary adventure.

Eventually, I began entertaining quite a lot, too. My friends would help me in the kitchen, and gradually I began to develop my repertoire, which was simple: Mostly, I would grill things and serve them with a big green salad and perhaps a vegetable gratin. I'd serve pâté with thin slices of French bread as an appetizer, with some olives. It was all easy, but soon I developed more confidence in my cooking and entertaining. Through Elizabeth David and my husband, as well as Nina, I was becoming passionately interested in Provençal cuisine and Mediterranean flavors—light, clean, fresh flavors, olive oil, garlic, herbs. It spoke to me. I didn't feel the need to make Austrian dishes. The only thing, at this point, that I was really missing from Austrian cuisine was the pastries and the sausages. The Mediterranean cuisines rely so much more on the integrity of the original ingredients and to do very little to them; they bring out the natural flavor of the vegetables. Many of our single women friends would stay with us for weeks when they felt lonely or were between boyfriends, and every evening became a gathering with good food and company.

The more I cooked, the more I was on the lookout for fresh, inexpensive ingredients. I began discovering and shopping at ethnic markets, including a nearby Asian grocery. I had no idea what most of the ingredients were—there were strange dried fish that smelled like old socks, vegetables I didn't recognize, and bins of herbs and roots—but I knew that I wanted to learn.

· · ·

One day, I saw a flyer for an Asian cooking class posted at the store. Pierre had loved Asian food from the time he lived in Vietnam, and I wanted to expand my repertoire. The class was not expensive, so I signed up.

At the first class, there were only four of us, plus the daughter of the store owner, standing around a table in a tiny kitchen at the back of the store. She took us on a tour of the ingredients in the store, holding each one up and explaining what it can be used for. I was used to powdered ginger but had never smelled the aroma of the freshly grated root, nor could I tell the difference from galangal. I had never tried lemongrass, with its delicate flavor. Over the next few weeks, I tasted crunchy bean sprouts, silky tofu, aromatic cilantro, bamboo shoots, water chestnuts, star anise, and all kinds of new flavor combinations and ways of cooking. I couldn't wait to get home to experiment with all these new flavors and recipes.

One day, we learned a foolproof way to cook a chicken evenly. "I'm going to teach you how to make boiled chicken without boiling it," the teacher told us. She brought out a stockpot and filled it with light chicken broth.

"You could also just use water with some seasoning and vegetables," she said. She seemed so casual and confident while she was cooking. She showed us how you then take a whole chicken, rinse it off, and put a metal spoon and a piece of ginger inside the cavity.

"What is the spoon for?" I asked. The teacher gave me a look that said I should be patient. Then she dropped the chicken in the pot, brought it back to a boil, covered it, then turned off the flame. Fifty minutes later, she pulled out a perfectly cooked chicken—moist, tender, and delicious. The spoon had conducted the heat evenly throughout the chicken, so it was moist and tender. I still use this method today.

Another surprise: she then removed the skin and pulled the meat apart for chicken salad. Wasn't this defeating the purpose of cooking a whole chicken? I thought. Why go to all that trouble just to shred it? Then I realized that meat was not the centerpiece of the meal, surrounded by vegetables, but something that could last for many meals. By adding glass noodles and vegetables to it, you could turn one chicken that would normally feed perhaps four people into a meal for a dozen. Given our circumstances in those days, I was keen to learn recipes that not only were unusual and tasty but would stretch to several meals.

I experimented and cooked more and more. I had fallen in love with cooking, and Pierre and I both loved all our socializing and wonderful meals. He was pleased that I was becoming a good cook, and friends complimented me on my food. After a couple of years, Pierre suggested that I try to find a job to help with his income. We could barely afford a car, and we definitely couldn't travel back and forth to Europe to see our families.

Although I had spent a year in a business school in Vienna and then a couple of years at a technical college, I did not have a degree or practical experience. I did speak French and German, however, so I interviewed at the World Bank. The job sounded terribly depressing. I would be expected to sit in an office typing all day long, only to occasionally find lodging or sightseeing tours for visiting German delegations. If the mere job description was stultifying, I couldn't imagine doing it day in and day out.

In the middle of the interview, the boss, a middle-aged woman in a suit, stopped what she was saying and looked at me. There was an awkward moment of silence as I realized I had tuned her out and was only focused on how dreadfully beige and boring the surrounding office was and how much I would hate having to sit at a desk and wear one of those suits with low pumps, smiling at everyone who needed something from me, no matter how much I resented being there.

"You're so young, and you're already married," she said. "You should start a family and enjoy it. You shouldn't be working in an office." I was taken aback: I might have been thinking this, but who was she to tell me how I should live my life? Why did she think young women shouldn't be working? But she was right: raising children at home would be vastly more satisfying and enjoyable than this particular office job. Plus, it made more sense to focus on the family now and my career later when the children were off in school. I suppose she also sensed my disinterest, and I'm glad she didn't hire me.

But I was frustrated, not knowing where to turn. I decided I would go back to school to get my degree in interior design. I enrolled at the International Institute of Interior Design and took classes for an accelerated diploma. But I quickly became discouraged there, too; it seemed my career track would be to cut out fabric swatches in a furniture store, when I had much grander ideas, going into a home and transforming it into a palace. While the school was closed during the 1968 riots, after Martin Luther King Jr. was killed, I learned I was pregnant. It seemed right to stop for at least a while.

That summer, our group of friends decided to rent a beach house. The previous year, Alain and Danielle had rented one in Rehoboth Beach, Delaware. Over the summer, they invited several friends, mainly foreigners, including our dear friend Georges.

At the beginning of the season, we all arrived at the beach house on a Friday night and began discussing how we were going to organize things. Alain offered to take care of bringing cheese and wine; another couple volunteered to bring good fish; someone else offered to pick up produce. But it wasn't clear how we were actually going to get meals on the table.

Alain and Danielle looked at me.

"Nora," said Danielle. "Maybe you can be the person to organize the meals?"

I must have looked shocked, because Alain jumped right in.

"We'll help cook and bring groceries, of course, we just need someone to coordinate everything, and since . . ."

"Since you don't have a full-time job right now," Danielle interrupted, "we thought you could do that."

It almost seemed as if they'd discussed this in advance. "What a great idea," said Georges. "Nora will be perfect for that."

Pierre nodded, as did everyone else in the room, and

though I felt a little ambushed, I couldn't do anything but agree. It was true that I was the only one who didn't have a full-time job. I didn't trust myself to come up with all the meals, but everyone reassured me that I made great menus at dinner parties and was involved with cooking the meals at the beach house anyway, and we needed an organizer. They'd shop and help cook; I just had to come up with the shopping lists and menus.

"Okay," I said, "I'll do it." I was nervous, but I couldn't tell my friends no.

This was my first experience organizing a set number of meals for a big group of people. Because I wasn't working, I stayed the whole week at the beach, while Pierre came and went on the weekends. I planned what we'd eat over the week-end and distributed the shopping list. I prepared as much as I could ahead of the time, and then finished things off with everyone's help at the last minute.

Everyone also had something he or she would contribute. Alain did the mayonnaise; he was a fanatic about making it properly. He cracked an egg yolk into a coffee cup, inspected it, then added a tiny spoonful of mustard and meticulously added drops of olive oil, one by one, all the while stirring vigorously, until the texture was perfect. Georges, of course, would often man the grill, cooking steaks for all of us.

I cooked simple dishes, often a beef roast with a potato gratin and roasted vegetables for Saturday night, along with a salad. Or I'd grill a butterflied leg of lamb rubbed with rose-mary and garlic and served with ratatouille, which I loved. The next day, I would take the leftover ratatouille, mix it with eggs to make a *piperade basque,* and then serve it with some thinly sliced ham. Other times, we would eat lobsters that had been shipped in from Maine and sold at the local grocery store. I was greatly enjoying myself! Once, when we had twenty lobsters, a friend suggested that we cook the lobster in the dishwasher with, of course, no soap. It worked brilliantly.

One day, someone suggested we have crabs for dinner, so we all piled in the car to catch crabs at Rehoboth Bay. We knew friends with a house there, so we went onto their pier with buckets full of chicken wings and cut-up squid. We tied them onto a line, dangled it off the pier, and within minutes a big blue crab clamped onto the bait. We netted the crab, threw it into the cooler, and caught some more. I spent days cooking crabs, making them into all kinds of different dishes, from crab cakes to bouillabaisse and chowder with bacon and potatoes. This was truly fresh and local food! I felt optimistic.

Alain worked at the Belgian embassy, and somehow he was able to trade barrels of red wine from the French embassy for Belgian endive and Belgian beer, so we always had plenty to drink. We collected any empty bottles we could lay our hands on—whiskey, gin, vodka, wine, whatever was on hand—and gathered at his garage in D.C. to pump the wine from the barrels and siphon it into the smaller bottles so that we could take wine with us to the beach house. Needless to say, we were all usually drunk from just the smell of all the wine by the time this process was over.

Once, on the way back to Washington, I got a ride with

Alain's wife, Danielle, and we were stopped for speeding. The policeman asked for her license. "Mon Dieu!" she said to me and turned pale. Her license was in her bag in the trunk, which was filled with empty wine bottles and stank of alcohol. This was long before the days when people recycled bottles, so it looked as if we'd had a nonstop party. We did not know what to do, and we were afraid he was going to arrest us. Danielle batted her eyelashes—she was a very pretty woman—and told the officer she somehow didn't have her license. When he told her she'd been driving much faster than the posted twenty miles per hour, she said, "I'm so sorry, Officer, my car just doesn't go that slow!" She drove a big Pontiac. She said something about diplomatic immunity and started speaking in rapid French, and the officer, frustrated, let us go.

After the summer was over, we continued to have dinner parties, but because our friends were used to my organizing all the food, they kept calling me, saying they had ten people coming for dinner, what should they cook? So I kept on helping: I planned their parties, I cooked for them, and sometimes I even got paid, albeit informally, to cook for friends of friends. I didn't consider it work; I loved to plan meals, and I loved to cook and entertain. It felt good to me that after only a few years I was no longer nervous about cooking for friends or even strangers and now my friends were looking to me for help with their dinner parties. Finally, after their initial generosity, I could truly reciprocate.

.   .   .

By the end of the summer of 1968, I was pregnant enough to have people stare at me in my bikini, but I felt wonderful and believed, as I do now, that pregnancy was nothing to hide. As my pregnancy progressed, I happened to talk with a pregnant friend of a friend who was even closer to her due date. I started asking her about her doctor and the hospital she'd chosen and how giving birth works in the United States. I really had no idea.

"I'm not going to a hospital," she said. This news surprised me; I didn't know there was any alternative. Remember, this was the late 1960s, and people had a very conservative approach to health. I asked her why.

"If you go to a hospital, you're treated like a number," she said. "You go in when you're in labor, they knock you out, and when you wake up, they tell you if you had a boy or a girl, but you can't see the baby, because they put it into another room." In the meantime, she said, they often have to use forceps during the birth because you're unconscious and can't help push the baby out, which can cause head injuries. "Because the mother is unconscious, she misses out on the first moments of bonding with her baby," she said.

It sounded dreadful—kind of like a supermarket atmosphere, sterile and impersonal—but I wasn't sure I was willing to take the risk of having a baby outside the hospital.

"Don't you want to be aware and awake when you give birth to another human being?" she asked me. "Don't you want your child to be in the best condition possible to start its life?"

I did want to be conscious, I decided. Of course I did; it

would be one of the most important moments of my life, and I wanted to be fully awake. She gave me the name of her obstetrician, Dr. Brew, who was the only physician in Washington, D.C., who would do home deliveries. When I went to see him, he examined me and said I was young and in good shape, so I was a good candidate for a home birth, and if I encountered any problems or abnormalities, I could still go to the hospital.

I asked my mother to come help for a few weeks around my due date and told her I wanted to give birth at home. She was horrified. "We women were fighting to be able to go to the hospital for childbirth, and you want to stay back home!" she said. I recalled that she had traveled, alone, hiking all the way down from the farmhouse in Tyrol to make her way to Vienna, just to have me in a hospital. She warned me that it was dangerous, but ultimately I knew she would support my decision.

The doctor recommended a nurse, who didn't live far away, to call when I was in labor. When my contractions started getting closer, I called the nurse, who came and examined me. She told me I was still a long way off and left to go shopping. This was before cell phones, and there was no way to reach her. By the time we finally got in touch with her, my labor was well under way, and when she arrived, the pain was so intense I felt I couldn't take it anymore. "I can't do this," I told her as soon as she arrived. "Give me something."

"I don't have anything to give you," she said.

"Just hit me on the head with a hammer and put me out!" I told her. I remembered from reading all the books on home birth that when you're in the last transitional phase—when, for example, you're ready to kill your husband for putting you into this situation—that means you're ready to push. Fortunately, the doctor came up the steps right then. I think I pushed Alexis out in about ten minutes. The doctor lifted him up, measured him with a sewing tape measure, and, because we had no scale, estimated he weighed about six and a half pounds.

I washed my face, put on fresh pajamas, and got back into bed, with my new baby at my breast. Alexis was born at around 2:00 p.m. By 4:00 p.m., my friends had come by to visit, all popping bottles of champagne. I felt so happy: I'd brought another human being into the world, and I'd been awake to do it and to feel the marvelous glow afterward of being with my husband, my mother, my friends, and my brand-new baby.

We had our second son, Olivier, twenty months later. This time, Dr. Brew was away on safari, but he had given us the name of another physician, an older woman who lived an hour away, who would do a home delivery. She agreed to help with the birth. The labor was easier the second time and seemed to go faster. I told Pierre to call the new doctor. When he came back from the phone, only a little while later, I told him I couldn't help it, I had to push.

I pushed a few times, and soon another son was born into Pierre's hands. I had him on my breast when the doorbell rang. Pierre opened the door for the doctor and exclaimed, "Doctor, it's a boy!" Not seeming to understand, she said, "Relax, I'm here, it will all go smoothly." Pierre shook his head. "It's a boy! Everything already went smoothly!"

The doctor examined me and looked at us, saying, "Well,

it's a good thing I came anyway, because you need me to write the birth certificate. Otherwise, your son wouldn't exist!" She filled out the birth certificate and left as our friends again came with champagne. I'd been so sure I was going to have a girl I hadn't thought of a boy's name, so I asked our friends. Georges said, "Why don't we call him Olivier? It sounds great with Pouillon." So we did.

After Olivier was born, we realized we had to find a larger house. We decided that it was time to buy, but it wasn't easy to find something we could afford. Eventually, we started looking in a neighborhood called Adams Morgan, which Pierre liked because it had an international feel. We found a completely ramshackle town house that was being used as a rooming house and bought it. The only problem was that it needed a lot of work.

The process of renovating was difficult, and much of it fell to me. It quickly became apparent that my husband was the furthest thing from a handyman. I had to do most of the fixing up and find people to help me—all while taking care of two small children, cooking, cleaning, and entertaining. I didn't feel that Pierre was giving me enough support, and it was a stressful time. He was essentially helpless in daily life, though he tried to be a helpful, loving father. I'm sure I became a less loving wife to him, and I felt less and less attracted to him and more resentful. And our sex life began to disintegrate.

My frustrations with Pierre's inability to help fix up the house were, of course, more deeply rooted. When I married him, he'd seemed so capable and worldly. I thought he would take care of me. I hadn't really listened when he said that he wouldn't be able to make much money in the United States, and I was too naive to understand the consequences. He was an intellectual and not a problem solver. It was becoming more and more clear to me that I was going to have to be the one to figure out how to make a better life for my family. Our relationship, not surprisingly, deteriorated.

We tried to revive our marriage by taking a vacation across the country. Antoine, Pierre's sister's son, said he wanted to do a tour of the United States with a friend. I asked our German friend Gudrun, whose son was the same age as Alexis, if she would stay at our house with the children, who were four and two, while we went on our two-week drive.

Our destination was California, and to get there, we had to go through all the *I* states—Illinois, Indiana, Iowa. They were huge and flat. I got anxious there: the farther into the middle of the United States we were, the worse the food became. We would survive on a big egg breakfast and then not eat anything until night, when we'd splurge on the best restaurant in town, where they served steaks that were so big they were hanging over the plates. The baked potatoes were enormous, filled with sour cream. Often there would be a huge salad bar, with nothing that resembled salad but things like shocking-pink and lime-green Jell-O salad with mayonnaise. I couldn't believe it. On top of that, many of the states were dry—no alcohol. There was definitely not any wine! Even if you could find alcohol, it was more often simply hard liquor. Washington, D.C., seemed very cosmopolitan by comparison with the rest of the country.

But we loved the scenery and national parks along the way. As a European, I had never seen anything like Bryce Canyon, with its orange hoodoo rocks and spires. Nor is there anything in Europe like the Grand Canyon, which we saw near the end of our trip. We didn't have time to hike all the way down, so we splurged and took a plane ride. We flew over what seemed an endless plain until we dipped down into the canyon, which was suddenly green with a high turquoise waterfall on the left. Yellowstone National Park also astonished me, with its shooting geysers and grizzly bears and bison lazily wandering around the aspen meadows.

Finally, after more than a week, we arrived in California. We went to Yosemite National Park, which, with its granite Half Dome and long waterfalls, took my breath away; I could have stayed there, hiking, the whole time. We stayed at the Ahwahnee, one of the better hotels in the park. We went to dinner and were so relieved: there were fresh vegetables, perfectly prepared, and a reasonable-sized steak. Pierre was in heaven because the wine list was extensive and introduced us to California reds. We also ate wild salmon, which was fresh and rare to find on a menu in Washington, D.C., or Europe. Similarly, when we reached San Francisco, we were excited to have so many different types of foods to try and spent most of our time wandering around, exploring all the Chinese, Japanese, and Mexican restaurants.

We'd had fun exploring the United States, but the truth was that for long stretches of the trip I was lying in the backseat, half-dead. I was depressed; I don't know if it was the endless, dull countryside or the fact that Pierre and I weren't getting along. Whatever else the trip did for me—discovering the United States and the marvelous food and drinking wine in California—it did nothing to improve my marriage.

When we got home, I was so busy renovating the house and taking care of the children that I needed help. My sister had a friend whose daughter wanted to come to the United States to improve her English. I liked the idea of having someone else to speak German with, and I was thrilled about having help with the house and the children, so I said yes. So Ditte, the au pair, arrived, and it turned out she was very nice. She was also beautiful: her mother was a Brigitte Bardot–type actress, and Ditte was simply a younger version. When, one evening, I saw Pierre flirting with her, I became alarmed. Our relationship was already on the rocks. I knew he was charming and that the presence of this young woman could mean trouble.

"Look," I told him one evening, "I can take you having an affair with anyone else, but don't do it with her."

Pierre rolled his eyes, as if I were paranoid just to be thinking that.

"I mean it," I said. "Not only is she too young, but how do you expect me to ask her to be helpful in the household and take care of the children if she's just rolled out of your bed? If she's too tired to bring the kids to school because she's exhausted from having sex with my husband all night?"

"Okay, okay," Pierre said. "Of course I won't do that." He waved away the idea, as if I were crazy.

Not long afterward, my sister wrote to tell me that the au pair had confessed to her friend that she was indeed having an affair with Pierre. Ditte was young and impressionable, but even so she was still under my roof. And Pierre had completely broken my trust. I was furious—not so much that he'd had an affair, but that he'd given me his word that he wouldn't do so with Ditte. He'd lied to me.

One night, I woke at 2:00 a.m., and he wasn't next to me. Instead, he was taking a shower, which was not something he normally did in the middle of the night.

When he came back to the bedroom, I confronted him. He protested, but as I made it clear that I wasn't stupid, he admitted it. "Look," he said, "it's not my fault. She came to me."

I gave him another scornful look.

"Nora, you haven't wanted to; we haven't been intimate lately. What did you expect me to do?"

"I expected you not to sleep with the au pair," I said. "That's all I asked."

I was disgusted and disappointed, sad that our twelve years together had come to this. Pierre kept asking for my forgiveness, but it wasn't about forgiveness anymore. Our relationship, the trust between us, was fundamentally broken.

The next evening, after the boys were asleep, I left the house and walked all the way from Adams Morgan to Georgetown to visit Shelley. When I arrived, I was hiccuping with sobs.

"Nora, it hurts, but it doesn't have to be a big deal," Shelley said. "Lots of people have affairs, and most of the time it doesn't mean anything."

I shook my head. "It's not just the affair. It's that he promised. Not with the au pair."

Shelley gave me a hug.

"It's terrible that he promised you and broke his promise," she said. "But it's not important. You're the one he loves. Men do this. It's some kind of midlife crisis. He'll get over it. He loves you."

I walked back home, and on the way I made a resolution: if Pierre was going to do it, so was I. Why should men be able to sleep around while women look the other way? I wanted to get back at him.

When I arrived at the house, Pierre was relieved. He'd been worried about where I was. I acted as if we had made some peace, but I knew things weren't fixed between us.

I thought about my male acquaintances and tried to decide whether I could have an affair with any of them. I wasn't going to harm my circle of friends by sleeping with one of them. I finally decided the only interesting man who wasn't a personal friend was our contractor. He was practical and down-to-earth, a little stocky, but cute. He'd always been flirtatious with me. He was married, too, so we met in an apartment he rented downtown—a neutral place. We saw each other at lunch once or twice a week; I felt like Catherine Deneuve in a French film. I liked feeling desired again, that a man would think enough of me to take the trouble and expense to rent an apartment to meet with me. It gave me back some of my self-esteem after I'd felt terribly hurt by Pierre.

I was still frustrated at home—with my marriage and with

having no job. Even the dinner parties I loved to throw were beginning to seem tedious.

One evening, we were entertaining friends, including a woman named Sharon, who was a women's libber, as they were called then. She was very impressive; she was one of the first women to successfully sue the government when she found out that a man was making much more than she was for doing the same job. We were having drinks and a fun time when she pulled me aside.

"Nora," she said, "you're far too intelligent to waste your life like this, getting drunk every evening."

I was surprised by her comment. At first I was offended; I was fixing a house, making a home for my family, caring for my children, throwing dinner parties. I was plenty busy. But I began to realize that she was right: aside from my children, I wasn't doing anything in my life that was constructive—something useful, something that would make a difference outside my own home. This was the 1970s, and feminism was in full bloom, and it was a moment when more and more women—like so many of my professional friends—were finding interesting work, using their minds, doing jobs that made them feel challenged and fulfilled, being sexually free. I wanted—and deserved—something different, something new for myself, too. I couldn't just be a housewife, especially because my husband wasn't able to support us in the way I had hoped. I wanted more. I wanted to express myself and also to be financially independent.

I knew I wanted to try my hand at something I could feel

proud of, that I could create, develop, and call my own. I'd been frustrated and restless, and I needed a career with a purpose. Many of my friends were already consulting me about dinner parties and asking for my help. A lot of people, I thought, might need assistance figuring out how to feed their family on a small budget. I could create different menus that were simple and didn't take too much time to prepare. Everyone I knew was busy—women were working, cleaning house, and shuttling their kids around—and needed some quick, easy ideas to make dinners.

I had only taken one cooking class in my life, but I decided that I knew enough to be able to teach one myself. I had no idea what it involved, but I was young and optimistic, and this willful enthusiasm—and perhaps naïveté—allowed me to move forward without thinking too much about the steps it would take to do so.

I got organized. I put flyers around the neighborhood and in the supermarket for what I chose to call "Low-Budget Gourmet" classes, which I held in my house. My idea was to show how, for fifty dollars, you could feed a family of four for five dinners and one or two brunches.

Very soon, the classes filled up. First came friends from the neighborhood—people who had been to my dinner parties and liked the food I cooked. Then came friends of friends and then strangers—women who responded to the flyers. I held the classes in my kitchen, which was big enough to fit nine chairs. In the middle of the room, I set up a couple of card tables and covered them with an oilcloth, which was where I demonstrated the techniques and invited my students to help me.

Each week, we would have an evening class based on a protein, which was whatever was on sale at the local supermarket. One week, chuck steaks were on sale, so I had a beef class: you'd grill the steaks one day, then make a salad out of the leftovers the next day, a ragout another day, and then put the ragout leftovers into a pasta sauce with lots of vegetables the day after that. I did the same with chicken, which was very popular. I showed my students how to buy three chickens, bone them, make a stir-fry out of the chicken breast one day, stuff and roll the boned breasts on another, then roast the legs the next evening or cut up the legs to make a chicken marengo or cacciatore. We'd make a little pâté appetizer out of the livers with the addition of some cream cheese, and a Hungarian stew with lots of mushrooms, sour cream, and paprika, along with the gizzard. We'd also make a delicious chicken stock out of the bones and carcass that you could then serve with noodles and vegetables for lunch the next day. Throughout, we drank wine from my gallon jug and then ate dinner together at the end. It felt like a family meal—sharing food together, around the table, nibbling on French bread, drinking wine. Even today, many of these students are still friends of mine and regular patrons at my restaurant.

I thought I was an amateur cook, but I was truly amazed at how comparatively little my students knew about food. Some of my students didn't know how to boil an egg. They'd only eaten iceberg lettuce and had no idea that you were supposed to wash it before eating or that it was possible to make salad dressing yourself. Many of them told me that their mothers had never cooked and that they usually brought home Chinese carryout or ate fast food. Some just opened cans of spaghetti, and almost no one had cooked anything but Minute rice. To them, everything I said was a revelation. They'd really never been exposed to cooking—which is why they came to class and why I was glad to be teaching them.

The classes were a big hit, not only because my students were eager to learn these low-cost cooking techniques, but because we had a lot of fun. The classes didn't make much money, but they were a solid first step toward independence and gave me the assurance that I was good at something that people valued and that I could share. They made me realize that I might be able to support my family on my own—that I could be independent. I also realized that my friends would support me in whatever I did, for which I've always been grateful.

Pierre took care of the children while I gave the class, then he came downstairs and shared the meal with all of us once the kids were in bed. Given the tension in our marriage, I liked having other people around for dinner; it made it easier for everyone.

Not long after I began the classes, a friend who worked for the neighborhood paper called *Earthworks* asked me if I would write a column. She wanted to call it the "Guerilla Gourmet" and thought it would help my little business along. I was happy to oblige.

The cooking classes gave me a renewed impetus to find good local ingredients, and I began to search out more good ethnic shops in Adams Morgan. In the early 1970s, the neighborhood was incredibly diverse—a third African American, a third Latino, and a third sort of bohemian, with left-wing journalists like Carl Bernstein and John Marks, along with the health advocate Sid Wolfe. It was a very vibrant neighborhood, known for its internationalism, as were its markets.

One of my favorites was the Middle Eastern market around the corner from me, where the owner, Joseph, often invited me to lunch. I would bring Olivier in his stroller—Alexis was in preschool—and have a simple meal with him. He would cut up feta cheese, sprinkle olives and zatar around it, then pour good olive oil on top. He'd squeeze half a lemon over the whole thing, heat up some pita bread in the toaster oven, and make a marvelous lunch.

I still went to the Italian grocery store and the French market, and I also discovered an African American market, which sold chitterlings, pigs' ears, different sausages, collard greens, and kale. There was also a Latin American market that sold tortillas, *queso fresco,* black beans, and large bunches of cilantro. I had never cooked with these ingredients before, and I loved them. Each time, I was excited to find a new market, and a new cuisine, and to chat with the owner about how to make dishes with these new ingredients.

I talked about all my shopping adventures at dinner parties. My friend Larry Stern, who was an editor at *The Washing-*

ton Post, told Bill Rice, who was editor of the style section, that I was a real connoisseur of the Adams Morgan markets. One day, Bill called and asked if he could follow me around.

"Why would you want to do that?" I asked. I couldn't imagine why they would want me to be in *The Washington Post.* I refused at first, but my friends, as they have so often throughout my career, encouraged me to do it and gave me the support I needed to take a step forward.

Bill Rice came and interviewed me, and I took him on a walking tour of the markets in the neighborhood and introduced him to all the vendors I'd gotten to know. He wrote a wonderful article, with a photograph of me, with my hair permed into a kind of Afro, wearing bell-bottom jeans and platform shoes. The article was a step toward my becoming more visible and professionally secure, and I began to think I could make some kind of a career out of my cooking classes. So I started a small catering business called Food for Friends and got my first few jobs—including one with Ralph Nader. I remember that I overcooked the meat terribly—because it was grass fed, it was very lean—and I didn't charge them, in the end, because I was too embarrassed. But luckily, Ralph Nader still comes to the restaurant today, so clearly he has forgiven me!

It was right around this time that I had my first adventure buying organic meat from Mr. Koenig.

This was the first time I realized that the agricultural practices in the United States were different from what I was accustomed to—that I needed to do more research to find out where the food I was eating was being grown and how it was being raised. I began to become aware that making the same food available year-round—regardless of season or provenance or quality—didn't make much sense.

It was also the first time that I started to make a real connection between what we eat and how we feel. It was my encounter buying meat from Mr. Koenig that made me decide I wanted to find out more. What did it mean for, say, the chicken I was roasting? It came from Perdue, in a package. But what did that mean—what sort of horror story was taking place in the henhouses? Or what about the pork I ate? Or what about the vegetables—were they being sprayed with chemicals? How did they always look the same, anyway? Was it really safe to eat them? This was the point in time when I began to ask questions.

My cooking classes, I decided, had to be about more than how to make meat stretch for five days. They also had to teach people about the importance of cooking with natural, healthy food—food grown without chemicals.

My search for ingredients expanded from ethnic markets to ones that sold natural local produce—Stone Soup, Fields of Plenty, Yes! Organic Market, and other health food stores that were just beginning to sprout up. And I knew that whatever my next step would be, it would go beyond just cooking and focus on healthy eating.

CHAPTER 6

Tabard Inn

One evening, at the end of a cooking class, while we were finishing a glass of wine, I was cleaning up when one of my students approached me. She was a regular, an enthusiastic student who hadn't been able to boil an egg when she first walked into my kitchen.

"Nora, I don't know if you'd be interested, but I have a friend who just bought an officers' service club near Dupont Circle who wants to turn it into a bed-and-breakfast," she told me.

I wasn't really paying attention; it was the end of the day, and I was tired from a full day of family life, followed by teaching class.

"Her name is Fritzi Cohen, and she and her husband, Edward, bought this place in Dupont Circle," my student continued. "They're looking for someone to open a restaurant there. I told her you'd be perfect. I want you to meet her."

I put down the sponge and turned to her. "That's very nice," I said. "But I'm a housewife who teaches a couple of cooking classes out of my kitchen, that's all. I have no professional experience. I wouldn't even know where to begin."

She shook her head. "You'd be great. Just talk to her."

The next day, Fritzi called and explained that she hoped the new restaurant would be unusual and exciting. Everyone at the time was doing stiff, formal French cuisine, but she'd heard that I was cooking interesting Mediterranean food—Italian, Moroccan, and provincial French food. "I've heard wonderful things about your cooking classes," she said. "You are just what I'm looking for." She explained that she needed someone to install the kitchen and run the restaurant in the hotel; it would be my own business, giving her a percentage of the gross sales, so I'd be my own boss, but without any sort of significant capital up front. She already had someone who could help with the front of the house, as well as the bookkeeping; I was just going to be responsible for the food. "Would you be interested?" she asked.

"No thanks," I replied. "That would be impossible." Her enthusiasm was infectious, though, and the idea was intriguing. After hanging up, I wondered whether I'd said no too quickly. I admitted to myself that running a small restaurant actually sounded sort of appealing—an extension of what I'd been doing but in a more official capacity. But even though my boys were six and eight, already in school at this point, would I be able to take care of them if I took this position? I knew it would be more than a full-time job; it would consume my entire life. It would be crazy. With my cooking classes, I was able to manage things. I was with the children during the day after they came home from school, then Pierre took care of them during my classes a couple of nights a week. Running a restaurant would be a much, much bigger commitment—at least that much, I knew. Plus, I had no professional cooking or business experience whatsoever. I would have absolutely no idea where to start in opening a restaurant. Where would I get the ingredients? How much would I order? How would I find a staff? There were a million details I didn't know.

Over the next couple days, I thought it over. I'd been married for twelve years, and it didn't look as if Pierre were ever going to be able to earn much more than he was making. He had reached the top pay grade he could achieve in the government without becoming an American citizen, which he refused to do. People he had hired and who had become citizens were now working in superior posts. We argued over it—in order to marry him, I became a French citizen, though I remained an Austrian citizen as well—so why shouldn't he become an American? Our lives were here. But he was stubborn. He insisted on remaining French.

I knew now that I couldn't be financially dependent on him anymore; I needed to earn my own way. Even though we still lived together, even though we shared the responsibilities of raising our children, our marriage was falling apart. We were both having affairs. And I knew that however much in love I had been with him at twenty, now, at thirty-three, I could see that we had reached a dead end.

Undecided about my marriage and my future, I began to experience something akin to panic attacks. I couldn't sleep. I would wake up in the middle of the night, unable to breathe, thoughts racing through my head. I was afraid I was losing my mind. Finally, I went to see a psychiatrist.

It was strange to sit in an office and tell my story to a man I'd never met, but it was also a relief. The truth was that several years earlier my sister Rosi had been diagnosed as manic-depressive. I was afraid that the same thing might be happening to me.

Rosi had told me about her panic attacks and how difficult it was to get out of them. She wouldn't feel like herself. She'd have a manic phase, where she couldn't stop her brain from going around and around, without any chance to relax. Then she'd have a depressive phase, where she could barely get out of bed and was consumed by dark thoughts tormenting her.

I was very worried about Rosi—and fearful of her illness. After she'd left home, she'd gone to Paris and found work as a model. She'd always been tall and thin, beautifully elegant, with lustrous hair and skin, great lips, and shiny, straight teeth. She'd become a model for a big couturier house, doing photographs and fashion shows. Modeling was much different back then, though. There were no supermodels, and few women made much money. You were more like a "mannequin," as they called them. Rosi modeled for three years and was under the constant stress of starving herself—you had to be skinny then, too—and making enough money to live. Vati didn't support her anymore. At some point, it all became too much for her, and she had a nervous breakdown. Mutti had to go and pick her up from the hospital, where they'd been treating her with electroshock therapy, which horrified me. Mutti brought Rosi home, where at least she was more stable, and she eventually got a job translating business letters and went to art school on the side to paint. She seemed better for the moment and had married a quiet, amiable Finnish man; it was a good situation for her, finally. But she remained fragile. The thought that I could potentially go down the same road, because I knew mental illness ran in families, terrified me.

The psychiatrist listened while I explained everything that was going on in my life. Then he was very blunt with me. "The anxiety you are feeling stems from your relationship with your husband," he said. "You have two choices. Either you leave him and start your own life, or you try to work it out with a psychiatrist." Because I couldn't afford a psychiatrist on a regular basis, he suggested group therapy as an option, but I could tell he thought the best route would be to leave Pierre. These days, therapists are rarely so direct, but in this case I'm glad he gave me that advice. He reinforced my decision to build a new life for myself on my own terms.

All around me, women were working, having careers, leading creative lives without being financially tied to their husbands, or to their children and their homes. All the messages of the feminist movement, the way that women I knew were stepping out and claiming equality, really resonated with me. Women were encouraged to be self-sufficient and not depend on men. I wanted to be able to support my family. I wanted to make my children proud of me, to set them a good example. I wanted to be part of that revolution—in the world and in my own life.

This, then, was my big opportunity to do something on my own.

It was difficult for me to tell Pierre about my decision to take the job at the Tabard Inn. One evening, I finally mustered enough courage to explain that I'd come to the realization that he couldn't support me and the children and that I didn't want to be a burden on him. I had decided to take the job of running the restaurant in order to make a living for myself.

"You're going to have to take care of the children," I told him. "During the day, they are in school, and they can go to the after-school program as well. I'll be around during the weekends. But I'm going to be working long days."

Pierre was shocked. He ran his fingers through his hair and gave a loud sigh. "Nora," he said, "can't we figure something else out?"

I opened my hands, helplessly. "This is what I'm good at," I told him. "This is what I want to do, what I need to do."

He considered that. "Can I do the restaurant with you? Can we do it together?" For all of our problems, I could tell that he was still desperate not to lose me.

I shook my head. Pierre would be hopeless at running a restaurant. He would sit around smoking cigars and drinking wine and chatting with the guests, never doing so much as bringing a dirty plate from a table to the sink, much less organizing a kitchen, writing a menu, managing staff, and doing the payroll and accounting.

"You've made up your mind, then," he said wearily.

I nodded. "Pierre," I said, "I'm sorry. But I think it's the only way."

I called Fritzi and told her I would take the job. She was thrilled and said she'd hoped I would reconsider. From the start, I told her I would only do it if I could serve my kind of food. I wanted to use olive oil instead of butter, brown bread instead of white. I wanted fresh produce, in season, from local farmers, and I wanted a menu filled with whole grains and simple, tasty Mediterranean dishes. I wanted meat that had not been treated with antibiotics and hormones—beef that hadn't been fed corn and had been grazing freely. I expected some resistance—I was basically telling her I wanted to make natural, flavorful hippie food, as far as most of the world was concerned—but she immediately agreed, and we began making plans.

I went to the Tabard Inn to meet with Fritzi and her husband, Edward. The inn was a bed-and-breakfast near the White House, walking distance from *The Washington Post,* and close to Dupont Circle, with a cozy lounge area and a leafy, brick-walled garden. It was a bit of a dump, but in its own way it was cute and funky, and the garden was lovely, and I thought I could work with it. Right away, I liked the casual and homey feel of the place. But from the moment I met Fritzi and Edward, I knew this was going to be an enormous challenge. I would have to learn quickly. Fritzi, Edward, and I went over the details of what I would need to do: create a menu, build a kitchen, and at the beginning serve breakfast and lunch (dinner service came later). We also went over details of my contract, which, because I was inexperienced, I accepted without question. They also introduced me to Margaret, a young woman Fritzi wanted me to partner with. Margaret had experience running Christmas-season markets, so she knew, at least a little, how to operate a business. She would be the hostess and dining room manager.

As we walked through the hotel, I saw a young, short man with curly hair. He was wearing a bright orange raincoat and had just come in from trying to fix a leak on the roof of the inn. His hair was black and glossy from the rain. Fritzi introduced him as Steven Damato, the manager of the hotel who, luckily, was also very handy. He would help put the kitchen together. We shook hands, and I was struck by his firm handshake. He seemed to radiate energy with his bright blue-green eyes. He immediately jumped in, talking about plans for the kitchen, and I liked how competent and confident he seemed. As Steven left the room, Fritzi finished explaining the deal. The only thing I needed was a minor amount of starting capital; she and Edward would finance the construction of the kitchen, but I would need enough money for at least a month's worth of food and staff salary. I would also have to give them 20 percent of my gross sales each month, with no additional income from the bar. I knew this didn't seem right, but I also knew that it was a rare chance—that I was being handed a training period on a silver platter and that another opportunity like this might not come along.

So I asked Pierre for the money. It was not that much; I think Margaret and I had to come up with two thousand dollars each. Of course, back then, that seemed like a huge sum to me. Pierre, after his initial resistance, was very supportive and gave me the funds, which he had to borrow against his life insurance. "Go for it," he told me. "I'll pull my share and take more care of the children." He was truly a generous man and wanted to help me, even though I was not with him anymore.

The next day, I stepped into a professional kitchen for the first time, as the chef of my own restaurant.

The first thing I did, even before renovating the kitchen, was develop my menu. Breakfast was easy, because I would simply take over serving the standard continental breakfast available at the inn. It offered hard-boiled eggs and good flaky croissants that a baker delivered, to be eaten with jam, as well as some fruits and fresh juices. The inn already had suppliers for all these things, so that gave me a good head start.

Lunch was the greater challenge. I knew how to cook for a crowd, but daily for a restaurant? I had to teach myself how to order ingredients using simple math: If one person drinks two tablespoons of milk in his coffee, how much would five hundred people drink in a week? If I make twenty roast beef sandwiches a day, and each has three ounces of meat, how much roast beef do I need to order? It was not difficult, but it was a learning process. Everything was.

But for all its difficulties, lunch was also where I could be creative. I was nervous, at first, developing a restaurant menu, but I realized I could just make the same foods I'd cooked at dinner parties and in my cooking classes with a lot of success. They would be simple foods with a fresh twist. I developed a lot of sandwiches—a cold roast beef sandwich, BLTs, pâté sandwiches, roast pork sandwiches. But the cold roast beef sandwich had my homemade mayonnaise, which was much more flavorful than anything you could ever find at the grocery store, paired with Dijon mustard, sliced cheddar cheese, and romaine lettuce. I served my pork sandwiches with an Austrian-style cabbage salad that was much lighter than the coleslaw most delis served. My pâté sandwiches were served with homemade pickles. I found a bakery that made whole wheat and pumpernickel breads, so I didn't have to use the awful white bread most supermarkets sold.

With every simple salad and sandwich I created, my mantra was to make it from scratch and to use the freshest ingredients. Because of that, something as well-known as a BLT was a revelation to my customers when it had great, juicy Virginia tomatoes, toasted rye bread, homemade mayonnaise, crispy natural bacon, and romaine lettuce instead of iceberg. I served a *niçoise* salad, which no one in the United States had heard of at the time, unless they had been to France. I became known, too, for my curried chicken salad. Without realizing it, I had been picking up bits and pieces here and there, through my travels and my cooking classes and my reading about food.

Once I had my menu in place, it was time to start installing the kitchen. Having just renovated my house on my own, this felt like familiar territory, but at least this time I wasn't doing it alone. From the beginning, Steven was a big help. I came up with the basic design for the kitchen. I knew I wanted a big worktable, two ovens, and a gas stove with six burners, as well as lots of refrigerator space. It was very basic. Steven had worked in restaurants in Vermont, so he came up with a lot of helpful suggestions. I was so impressed by the way he took my ideas and turned them into a reality. I couldn't help feeling attracted to Steven, even though he was nearly thirteen years younger than I. For the first time in a long time, putting together that kitchen, I felt as if I were having fun, and if we were flirting a little, well, that was fun, too.

Fritzi redecorated the dining room, which was on the lower level of the inn. Cute and eclectic, with black-and-white tiles on the floor and charming paintings and photographs on the walls, the dining room was very cozy. Eventually, Fritzi also fixed up the garden so that in good weather people could eat outside, which they loved. The kitchen took shape very quickly. When everything was installed, Margaret and I trained the staff. I had found a few people—a morning breakfast cook and a dishwasher, and another prep cook—to help me in the kitchen. We were ready to open. I was terrified the day before the restaurant opened. Of course, we had breakfast for the people staying at the inn, but I had no idea whether anyone would come for lunch. I was so anxious—what if nobody showed up?

The restaurant was very near *The Washington Post,* so I called my friend Larry Stern, who was the assistant managing editor there.

"Larry, I just opened the restaurant at the Tabard Inn," I told him. "Tomorrow will be the first day I serve lunch. Will you come so I know I'll have at least one customer?" Larry was wonderful. He rose to the occasion, and not only did he come, but he brought twenty people along with him. It was nearly overwhelming for me in the kitchen to serve them all at once—especially because of course people want to have their lunches fast to get back to work.

As luck would have it, the Tabard Inn quickly became a success. Everyone raved about the sandwiches and salads, and from that moment on we were busy. The restaurant became a hangout for both local and visiting journalists and other writers, as well as left-leaning intellectuals. Fritzi was a well-known antiwar activist, always fighting for some cause, and she drew like-minded people to her hotel. People would have lunch there or drinks in the evening in the lounge, which had sofas, a fireplace, and a piano. The inn became something of a salon.

While I was working to start the restaurant that summer, Pierre had taken the children to France. That made a lot of sense to us both; I could concentrate on the new business, he would take care of the boys, and we would both have time to breathe and assess our relationship.

In the meantime, Steven and I began spending a lot more time together. He not only helped me build the kitchen but was used to handling employees and helped me hire people to work in the kitchen and taught me how to manage them. Each time I ran up against a challenge, he was there to help. He didn't fix things for me; he fixed them with me, which was a huge difference. I never felt belittled; I felt as if he were teaching me a lot about running a restaurant and giving me the confidence to do things for myself. He spent a lot of time in the kitchen, checking on how everything was working and then tasting whatever I was preparing. He loved my food, which also made me happy.

Every time Steven came in, I felt a little spark, a frisson between us. In some ways it was ridiculous: he was barely twenty-one, and I was a thirty-three-year-old married mother of two children. But we worked well together, and it was exciting to accomplish so much after my many years as a housewife. I felt as if I had momentum in my life, and he was helping me to fuel it. Steven was practical, hardworking, and ambitious. His physical energy was thrilling and sexy. He was the complete opposite of Pierre, and perhaps for that reason I was irresistibly drawn to him. It wasn't long before I found out that the feeling was mutual.

Because I was working long hours, with a breakfast serving at six, and because the Tabard Inn was quite a distance from my house—and given that Pierre and the children were away in France for the summer—I started staying overnight with Steven, who lived in a small apartment at the inn. We both thought that we were just having a summer fling; we were spending so much time together building the kitchen and opening the restaurant. To my surprise—and to his—we fell in love.

We became very close, and as the summer drew to an end, I realized that I could not go back to Pierre. I felt guilty and torn, because this meant that my relationship with my children, and my ability to spend time with them, would change. I had given them every hour of the first six and eight years of their lives. Now, as painful as it was, I knew that I needed to spend more time on my career. I also knew that I would have to rely on Pierre to take care of Alexis and Olivier day to day.

I called Pierre while he was still in France, staying with his sister on the coast of Brittany. I was surprised that my friend, and Pierre's coworker, Muriel answered. *Of course,* I thought, *now he's having an affair with her too.* As a result, I admit, it made it easier for me to tell Pierre that I would be leaving him.

When he got on the line, Pierre sounded surprised to hear from me.

I didn't waste much time. "Pierre, I'm calling because I wanted to let you know that I came to a decision," I said. "I think it's best for us that I move out of the house for a while."

He was quiet. "Are you sure that's what you want to do?"

"Yes," I told him. "When you come back to D.C., I will have moved out."

"But where are you going to go?"

"I'm moving into the Tabard Inn. I'm moving in with Steven Damato."

There was another pause. "But, Nora, I'm giving you the

space you need to do what you want to do, as we agreed," he said. "I've been trying to be supportive. What more can I do?"

"I've made up my mind, Pierre." There was no turning back.

"What do you want me to tell the children?" Pierre sounded very upset.

So I told him that when they returned, we'd all go on a trip together, and I'd tell the boys then. Pierre, to my surprise, continued to plead with me, to tell me that I didn't need to do this, to end things. He wanted to talk about it in person. So I agreed that we wouldn't end things yet and that we could keep talking but that after our trip we'd have a trial separation for six months, and then we'd see how we felt.

Pierre was unhappy, but that's how we left the situation. When he came back from vacation, we took the children to the Outer Banks, to Ocracoke, North Carolina, for a few days. We'd spent happy times there before, but now, even though we spent many hours talking, we were at an impasse. While we were there, I told the children that I had started a restaurant and because of my work I wouldn't live in the house anymore. I assured them I would be living close by so they could easily visit me, and I would see them on weekends or whenever they wanted. I explained that Pierre would take care of them at home.

Olivier was too young to understand what that meant, but Alexis was very upset. When I told him, we were walking on the beach, and he just stopped and looked at me. "Mommy, I wish you would never have done this restaurant." It nearly broke my heart.

Telling my sons what I was going to be doing, and then following through with it, was the hardest thing I'd ever done. I knew that the boys, at this age, couldn't possibly understand that it was necessary, both for me and for our family. If I could have done both—be a full-time mother and run the restaurant—I would have. But there was no way of doing the restaurant half-time, and this opportunity was a rare one. I needed it, or I was going to drown. Giving up time with my children was a brutal choice, and one that I had plenty of moments to regret in the years to come, but one that, ultimately, I knew then—and now—was right.

Pierre learned to cope with the children by himself, and the kids became closer to him. He took care of the house and learned to cook, and he always had friends, especially women, to help him out. Soon he had a serious girlfriend, and I moved to a house just around the corner from where he and the boys lived, so I saw the boys every weekend and whenever else I could. But Pierre was still upset about the whole situation, and he claimed he was still in love with me. He told me once that whenever I wanted to come back, he would have me.

None of my friends could understand why I had left Pierre for Steven. Many of them were used to being able to come stay with Pierre and me, to enjoying our long, wine-soaked dinner parties. Now they missed our camaraderie. They also liked Pierre, for his worldly charm, his kindness, and his conversation. In person, he was a lovely man, and they simply couldn't understand why that wasn't enough for me. Many of my friends felt that when we drifted apart, they lost both of us.

Nor could my friends understand my affection for Steven. Most were shocked and pulled away from our friendship because his personality was so different from Pierre's. Steven was energetic, direct, and had a big personality—with a big appetite to match. He could be abrupt and loud or confrontational, erupting in anger. He was passionate, opinionated, and sometimes brusque and rude. Where Pierre was always smooth, Steven was rough. From the start, our relationship was tumultuous. He let all his feelings out, and I held things in, often resenting his outbursts. But we worked well together for a long time.

My family, too, was shocked by the turn of events in my life. I think they were less surprised that things were rocky with Pierre than by the development that I had taken a job running a restaurant. To them, working in a restaurant was manual labor, not something genteel, something that their daughter—who'd had all the advantages of French school, dancing lessons, European travel, Viennese balls—should be doing. My parents were proud to have risen socially and financially over their parents. They were in the upper-middle class and could afford maids and gardeners. Even so, they had never visited me at my restaurant and hadn't seen it for themselves. For me to be doing manual work was something they couldn't understand, and they were embarrassed to tell their friends.

I made new friends of my own through the Tabard Inn. One of them was Maya Miller, who lived upstairs. She'd worked out an arrangement with Fritzi where she turned the attic into a cozy apartment. Maya, from the start, was one of my biggest supporters. She saw what I was doing, taking a big step from being a housewife to running my own business, and she cheered me on. Maya was a feminist in her late sixties, with bright blue eyes and a dry sense of humor. She had lived in Nevada, on what was once a dude ranch, until she got divorced from her philandering scientist husband. Instead of moping, she took the energy and experience she'd gained from volunteering for different political organizations and ran for the Senate. I was amazed at the idea of a woman doing such a thing. She lost to Harry Reid, but she made quite a splash. After her defeat, she moved to Washington, D.C., and started the Women's Campaign Fund. She was energetic and political, loved good food and wine, and was extremely supportive of my efforts to serve natural food and to become independent. Maya knew that Steven and I didn't have much money, so she treated us to dinner at a variety of upscale restaurants so we could understand our competition, which was a lot of fun.

I also began to cultivate relationships with local farmers. From the time I opened the Tabard Inn, I knew I wanted to use the freshest, most natural ingredients. So, thinking back on my experience with Mr. Koenig, I became determined to find produce from local farmers. I drove around the countryside in Virginia and, one day, came across the Potomac Vegetable Farms, run by a Chinese Hawaiian woman who had been growing her fruits and vegetables with sustainable agricultural practices; she was determined to get away from using pesticides. She was growing arugula before anyone even knew what arugula was! She had all different varieties of tomatoes—

yellow tomatoes, plum tomatoes, cherry tomatoes. And such beautiful corn! I began to drive out to her farm in the summer at least once a week to get fresh herbs, salad greens, and all the other assorted vegetables I could find from her. When I think about it now, I realize that what I was doing was seeking out local produce, understanding that if I knew where it was grown and who was growing it, then I was more likely to find better fruits and vegetables—and that buying local was always the better option.

Soon, a small article was published in a Virginia farm journal about the restaurant, explaining that there was a restaurant in D.C. using local produce. Then more farmers began to come to me. It's hard to imagine now, but there were no restaurants in the area, or perhaps even the country, that were interested in buying local, pesticide-free produce. The vegetable farmer at the Rock Garden, a hippie commune, contacted me, saying he farmed organically and wondered if I'd like to buy his vegetables. I drove out to his farm in West Virginia, which was lovely. I told him what I'd like him to grow for me, and I agreed to buy all he grew in advance. It was an arrangement that worked well for both of us. I still have the same agreement with my farmers today.

Then the owner of Garnett Farms, Steve Garnett, who raised cattle for beef, called me and explained that he had worked for the Department of Agriculture and had bred a type of beef that was raised more naturally, without the use of hormones and antibiotics, unless the cows got very sick. They were all grass fed, finished off with some grain. I went to visit the farm, which was picturesque and clearly well managed; I thought, *I wouldn't at all mind eating beef that had been raised in that environment.* During my visit, Steve's parents told me their story. Mrs. Garnett was in her seventies at the time. She told me that she'd had a tumor the size of a baseball in her body, and after its removal and rounds of chemotherapy and radiation she attended a support group in which all of the other people were sick and had lost their hair. But she had made herself a broth with the bones from their own natural beef, which she drank all day long instead of water. She said she was never sick and never lost her hair. She believed she'd managed to fare so well because the broth had helped her develop her immune system so that it was strong enough to survive those chemical treatments. She felt that she was an example of what better meat could do for your body—that the women undergoing similar treatment in her support group had terrible side effects, but she had come through it feeling okay, and she attributed it to what she was eating.

I didn't know what to make of her story, but I couldn't help feeling that what she said made sense, and certainly it confirmed my belief that eating meat raised without antibiotics and hormones is better for you. So I bought their beef, and they, subsequently, told neighboring farmers that I was looking for pork, chicken, veal, and lamb of the same quality. I developed a whole network of suppliers from whom I could buy meat. I was pleased that my business could help to sustain their efforts to raise healthy animals and keep their farms up and running.

My supply of natural food, and my relationships with farmers, developed quickly, until a good portion of my menu—the meat, the vegetables, the fruits—was locally produced. This was 1977, and mine was one of the first seasonal, local farm-to-table restaurants.

Soon, one of my customers told me there was a woman named Alice Waters in Berkeley, California, who was doing something similar to what I was doing. I was extremely pleased to hear this. It was nice for me to know that there was someone else out there who agreed with me, who realized that our food chain and food production system needed to be fixed. Both Alice and I were self-taught cooks, with strong European influences, and we were both driven to achieve our visions.

Alice had an enormous advantage, being in California, where you could get fresh, local produce at all times of the year. I was still dealing with a shorter growing season, not to mention East Coast businessmen and visiting politicians from the Midwest, who were used to big portions and heavy meals. But beginning then, and to this day, I've always admired Alice and her work supporting local food networks, as well as children's education about eating healthy, nourishing meals.

Fritzi soon pushed me to start serving dinner. I had been doing just lunch and breakfast for two months. When we added dinner, it became much more complicated, because dinner is a more uneven business: Some days, ten people would show up; other days, it was forty. You never knew, so planning was difficult. How much food did you buy? What sorts of meals did you plan?

I became increasingly stressed, working from dawn to exhaustion. To make matters more complicated, Margaret, my business partner, was pregnant. As the months went on, she was getting very big, to the point where people were offering her, the hostess, a chair—not the other way around. Just before the baby was born, Margaret decided to leave the restaurant for good. It was only after she was gone that I learned she'd never paid my sales taxes and that I owed three thousand dollars in back taxes. I was shocked and devastated: I thought she had taken care of all the business details. I didn't have the money, partly because my contract with the Tabard Inn, it turned out, had not been favorable to me. I was paying for everything that concerned the restaurant—the food and its staff—and giving the owners 20 percent of my gross, as well as all the profits from my bar business, which, I've learned, is the most lucrative part of the restaurant business.

I didn't know what to do: I'd been working crazy hours, I'd sacrificed my time with my children to build my career, and all I had to show at the end of the year was a three-thousand-dollar debt. It was Maya Miller who came to the rescue. I was, and remain, forever grateful for her generosity. Maya was a huge supporter of mine from the beginning, almost like a surrogate mother; she took great care of me from the time we began to run the Tabard Inn. She was supportive of Steven and me as a couple when everyone else was shocked by us. Perhaps she saw me as having been in a similar situation to her own, and that was why she encouraged me. But I will always be in her debt. It was a friendship that lasted for the rest of her life, until she died, at ninety, on a former dude ranch in Nevada, where I made it a point to visit at least once a year.

When my year's contract with the Tabard Inn was up, the Cohens, who understood that our arrangement hadn't worked out well for me financially, asked me to continue as a fixed employee of the hotel instead of running the restaurant as my own concession.

Steven's contract with the hotel was up, too. One evening, we got to talking about what to do next. An idea hit him, and his face lit up, excited.

"Why don't we open our own restaurant?" he said. "Why not start somewhere of our own? Be our own bosses? Have the opportunity to make more money this way? We know how to run a restaurant now. We can make it work."

I didn't know what to say. Just a year before, I had been a housewife who ran a small catering business and cooking class on the side. Then I was running a restaurant, having left my husband, who was caring for our children. Could I do it again—start from scratch, build something new?

But I loved Steven and knew we made great partners. He knew how to be a manager and boss and how to fix things, which left me free to be creative. It was crazy, I knew, to try to start our own restaurant. But it couldn't be any more difficult than what I'd accomplished in the past year.

"Okay," I told Steven. "Let's do it."

CHAPTER 7

Restaurant Nora

It was almost Christmas 1977, and the highways heading north along the East Coast were dusted with snow. I was driving Steven's big Buick—an old taxicab—all the way from Washington, D.C., up to Vermont. Alexis and Olivier were in the backseat, drawing pictures on the frosty glass, excited about a week of skiing and some time together.

The farther north we got, the more the houses thinned out, and the trees and hills took over the landscape. It reminded me of growing up in Austria. In the crisp mountain air, for the first time in a long while—after the hard work at the Tabard Inn, the breakup with Pierre, and the uncertainty of my future—I felt good. I had some time off, I was with my children, and I was starting a new adventure, a new restaurant with Steven and his brother Thomas, who was joining us as a third partner.

In the backseat, Alexis and Olivier grew restless. They were spending their first Christmas without Pierre—and with Steven, whom they hardly knew. At home, Pierre would be spending the holiday with his girlfriend. And Pierre and I were trying to do everything possible to make our separation easier on the children, to always be cordial to each other in front of them, and to remind them how much we loved them. I was pleased to be able to take the boys skiing, a pastime that we all loved.

We would be staying with Jeremy Dworkin, who had employed Steven a few years before at his small inn and had remained a good friend. Steven was going to join me after a couple of days, so we could put our heads together and come up with a business plan for our new restaurant. He was finishing up loose ends at the Tabard Inn, training his successor.

I'd already said my good-byes, and fortunately things ended amicably. Just after I'd finished telling Edward that I didn't want to stay on and that Steven and I were starting our own restaurant, a woman happened to stop by the inn with her résumé. She'd had quite a bit of experience as a chef in the South. I had coffee with her, and we talked about cooking. Soon we began to chat very frankly about being a female chef.

"How can a woman chef in this town get a decent executive position?" she asked. "Each time I go for a job interview, they want to put me in pastry or pantry. At home, I was an executive chef!" She was obviously competent, professional, and creative but had been told, time and again, that she wasn't good enough—because she was a woman. This, of course, was back when no matter how great women were in the kitchen, they were considered merely cooks, not chefs. Fortunately, Julia Child had come along with her *French Chef* cooking show and her wonderful joie de vivre, which was beginning to change the image of professional women in the kitchen. Cooking might have been the domain of women in the home, but in most restaurants it was still strictly men who wore the chef's toque. The European chefs were the worst about letting women into their kitchens. I was lucky to have been my own boss; I had never experienced this discrimination. I also thought back to my father's insistence that I make something of my life; I was not brought up to be a housewife. It was strange, because he expected this of my mother but not of his daughters, so I never felt that I was lesser than a man. I wanted to continue to do the same for others.

I broke into a smile. "You've come to the right place," I told her.

She looked thrilled. I introduced her to Fritzi and Edward, and right away she took over as chef, and the transition was very smooth. I was pleased that she wanted to continue working with the farmers I'd met. Since that time, I've always tried to help other female chefs, either by supporting them or by hiring them. I didn't work my way up the ranks of the kitchen the way many of them did, suffering sexism, belittlement, and abuse from higher-up chefs, but I certainly knew what it was like to struggle to have a career as a woman, to break free from the constraints of marriage and family, and to start my own business. And I knew how essential the support of my friends had been for me. I knew that I'd left the Tabard Inn in good hands.

Before I left, I'd already met Steven's brother Thomas, who

had just returned from the Dominican Republic, where he had worked on a coffee plantation while in the Peace Corps. Like Steven, Thomas was smart and energetic. Steven had told him about our plans for the restaurant, and because he was looking for work, he wanted to join us. Unlike either of us, Thomas knew all about the financial nuts and bolts of running a business, as he'd done the accounting for the whole plantation. Steven thought he'd make a great third partner.

I was hesitant. I had worked very hard to get to this point, and I had to help support two boys for the foreseeable future, so I felt I couldn't afford to give up part of my ownership. Steven said he would give half of his half to his brother, which was very generous. As it turned out, Thomas contributed so much that he soon became an equal partner anyway. But I appreciated their generosity and fairness, which has consistently characterized our business dealings. We made a verbal agreement. Then Steven suggested we go to Vermont to map out our business plan—to think about investors and our next steps.

So here we were in Vermont. Jeremy's house was a big, clapboard New England farmhouse at the end of a dirt road that snuggled into the snowy landscape near Magic Mountain. It was spacious, with a big stone fireplace and a well-equipped kitchen, which had a big wooden farm table in the middle. Jeremy loved to entertain, and I was glad to be back to cooking for friends and the children. I practiced the menu for our upcoming restaurant by preparing meals for guests. I made my favorites from the beach house years: roast beef and potato gratin; leg of lamb with flageolets; and many preparations of chicken—roasted, stewed, or stir-fried. Steven studied Jeremy's extensive wine collection, planning our cellar. Jeremy gave us essential advice about how to start our business, helped us with the legal end, and introduced us to several investors. We worked hard in Vermont, but we had a wonderful time being together and with friends. It reminded me of one of the essential reasons I wanted to open a restaurant: I love the sense of hospitality and warmth that comes from preparing food and eating with friends.

But it wasn't entirely easy. The kids were used to spending time with me and their father; this was the first time they'd spent any extended time around me and Steven. It was a transitional period for all of us. One afternoon, we were out skiing, and I guess I'd spent more time skiing with Steven than with the boys. Alexis, who was nine years old at the time, became furious with me. The slopes were icy, and Alexis had fallen down and decided he'd had it; he wanted to go home. He took his skis and stormed off. He was determined to walk home. I was distraught and worried, but Alexis made it home safely. Once I knew he was okay, it became my first indication that Alexis was more comfortable in nature than anywhere else. He has always loved to be outside and has a natural aptitude for finding his way; it's like second nature to him. I started to see my son as who he was.

After their Christmas vacation ended, the children went home; Steven and I stayed on. We did some cross-country skiing, because downhill was expensive, and Jeremy took us around to several famous inns and restaurants in Vermont. We were suddenly seeing restaurants in a very different light, studying their menus, wine lists, furniture, decor, linens, and service. We paid close attention to what made us feel comfortable and welcome in a restaurant. Every day we refined our idea of what we wanted our restaurant to be.

I had decided that the way I cooked should be representative of my new home: I was living in America's capital, where people from all over the world came to reside, and so I wanted to cook with influences from many cuisines. America was a melting pot of all different cultures, and so that was how I chose to cook. I'd also developed a fascination with American folk art—what people were creating with their own hands, like sculptures and quilts. I wanted the decor of my restaurant to reflect this inspiration, and so we began to conceive of an interior with folk art in mind.

In February, we came back to Washington, D.C., full of ideas but with little money and no place to live. One of Steven's friends from the Tabard Inn was house-sitting in Adams Morgan and invited us to stay with her until we found our own home, which was nice for me, because I was close to the children. After about two months, we found a small apartment a block away from Pierre and the boys. The apartment was really a big closet: a double bed just barely fit in the bedroom, and the kitchen was hardly big enough to turn around in. But it was a convenient place to land, and that was all that mattered.

While we were putting our plans in place, we were living

off Steven's unemployment. We needed more money just to pay for basics, not to mention to open a restaurant, so I filled in for a friend who was a short-order cook at a nearby bar—it could hardly be called a restaurant—Café Don. It was in a fairly seedy neighborhood, and the people who came in only wanted a drink and a burger or eggs—basically, something to sop up the alcohol.

However accomplished I was as a chef, I wasn't a very good short-order cook. I prepared the burgers to order, but I didn't know how to turn them out fast. People were always yelling and complaining that it took forever to get food, and they were right. Still, it was an education. The whole time I was there, wiping sweat off my face and rushing to keep up with the orders, I kept thinking how glad I was that this was not the kind of restaurant I was going to have. My kitchen wouldn't be a little sweatbox with no windows or air, and my food would be entirely different, clean and healthy, from this heart-stopping grease. I didn't want to be an employee in anyone else's restaurant, nor would I treat my own employees rudely. I'm sure that if I'd kept on there for more than a couple of months, I either would have been fired or would have left, throwing in my apron. But I knew it was temporary, and necessary, so I just kept on flipping burgers and dreaming about my own restaurant.

From February to August, Steven, Thomas, and I scoured the area around Dupont Circle for a place we could lease. This was a frustrating process. Everywhere we looked, either the landlords wanted far more money than we had, or the building needed too much remodeling, often with a tiny kitchen in the basement. I didn't want to be a mouse down in the cellar, sweating over a hot stove in a kitchen with no windows, while upstairs everyone else had all the fun. I wanted cooking to be more like entertaining for friends; I wanted to be able to be in the thick of it all.

We were ready to abandon hope when one day my son Alexis told me that his friend's father owned a restaurant in Dupont Circle. He was, Alexis said, in very bad health and could barely cook anymore. I loved that Alexis was so eager to help me. I was certainly following all the leads I could find, so I asked him which place he was talking about. I realized I knew the building; it was a Yugoslavian café on a corner in a residential neighborhood, called Café Lovćen. It was the only restaurant in the neighborhood, because in general the area was not zoned for businesses, but the restaurant was old enough that it had been grandfathered in as a commercial establishment. Journalist friends of mine hung out there sometimes for its great potato salad, spicy sausages (*ćevapčići*), and slivovitz, which is prune schnapps.

I went to the restaurant and realized it was on the same corner where I'd bought sandwiches as a student in interior design school, when it was a grocery store and deli. I ordered lunch and asked to see the owner, whose name was Boshko. He invited me to sit with him and chat over a glass of slivovitz.

"I'm thinking of starting my own restaurant," I said, looking around. "I don't suppose you know of anyone who wants to sell a restaurant?"

He took a drink of his schnapps. "I might know someone," he said. He sighed and lifted a gloved hand, explaining that he had a skin disease that was making it impossible for him to cook anymore. "I'm tired of running my own business, too. It's just too much work."

I nodded sympathetically.

"You'll see," he said. "It's a lot of work."

He told me he wanted to sell his business, and I calmly said that I'd have to discuss it with my partners, but inside I was overjoyed. It was perfect.

I ran home to tell Steven.

"The restaurant is just the right size!" I told him "It has a kitchen on the ground floor and an apartment upstairs."

He came back with me and agreed. We loved the location. The redbrick building had been constructed at the turn of the century and had a lot of history and character. An alcove downstairs had displayed vegetables. What had originally been the stables would become our main dining room; the open back area, which had housed the horses, would later become our enclosed patio dining area. The kitchen had been the butcher's shop. The original owners had lived upstairs in an apartment (which functions today as our private dining room and office space). The same family had owned the property since it was built. It felt comfortable and traditional—a perfect neighborhood spot.

(Years later, we would celebrate the ninetieth birthday of one of the family's nieces, who had lived for a time in the upstairs apartment. That evening, she dined in what had once been her living room, looking out at Florida Avenue, where she had once seen horse-drawn carriages ride.)

We knew we had to find a way to make it work. So we went back to Boshko, negotiated the buying of the lease, and agreed that he and his family could stay upstairs in the apartment for at least three months until they could relocate. During that time, we would have to come up with the money. Boshko took back financing for part of the lease and arranged for us to pay him monthly over the next few years, but we still had to raise a great deal of money.

Admittedly, we were naive; we thought we could just go to the bank and get a loan if we already had investors, but at the time banks considered giving money to restaurants something akin to making a loan to the Mafia. We were only able to get a small amount from a neighborhood bank after making a lot of promises about how good the restaurant would be for the neighborhood and how we'd send customers its way.

What we got from the bank, however, was just a fraction of what we needed. We looked around and realized we had to turn to our own families. So after much convincing, Pierre took out a home improvement loan on the house that we still owned together; I had to promise him I'd pay him back when we sold the house. Steven and Thomas persuaded their parents to refinance their own home.

We made the rounds of friends, too, and raised more funds. Maya Miller, who had been so generous with me at the Tabard Inn, invested the most. Another couple who invested— and whose influence turned out to be worth much more than the initial money—was Ben Bradlee, editor of *The Washington Post*, and his wife, Sally Quinn, who were friends with Larry Stern, who had introduced us, and who lived around the corner from the restaurant.

When we pitched the restaurant to them, they were eager to have a new place in the neighborhood. Sally only had a few words of advice to me. "Don't mention anything about being healthy and natural," she said. "That sounds so unappetizing. That sounds like hippie food. Just do good things. Do lots of pasta. People love pasta."

I definitely wasn't going to give up on my idea of serving healthy natural food, but I knew Sally had a point—that I shouldn't make the food sound healthy over appetizing. Still, I felt that if people had the opportunity to eat good food that was also good for them, they would return. I also wanted to create a place with an unpretentious atmosphere, a neighborhood place where they could congregate.

We signed the contract with Boshko on Christmas Eve 1978. We gave him the money, and he gave us the key, toasting the deal over a glass of slivovitz.

Steven, Thomas, and I decided to begin tearing the place up that very night. We were in a rush to open the restaurant, because we had to start to make money as soon as possible. We'd even brought some sledgehammers along to get started.

We had our work cut out for us. We had to transform a kitschy Yugoslavian restaurant into a place that would be much more simple and lovely. The dining room had a dropped acoustical ceiling. The walls were surrounded by plastic wall sconces, which were painted black to look like wrought iron. On the walls were enormous murals of the Montenegro coastline, painted in turquoise and black. The kitchen and especially the bathroom were in bad shape. We tore in that night and continued to work for the next month.

Our furniture and the decor were very simple. We wanted to call attention to the food and make the place comfortable. One of our investors had photographs of marketplaces from the South of France that we blew up to put on the walls. I wanted calico tablecloths to give it a country feel and went all over Washington buying yards of different fabric. Steven's mother sewed all our tablecloths and napkins. Steven bought a big old antique cash register to put behind the bar. We hired a line cook to help with salad prep, as well as a small waitstaff. At first, Thomas was the host, the bartender, and the accountant. I was the chef and did the recipe development and menu planning; Steven ordered the food and took care of the wine list and management. Soon we were ready. It amazes me today to think that we opened just over a month later, on January 30, 1979, for lunch and dinner.

The first day we opened, old friends from *The Washington Post* showed up. Ben Bradlee and Sally Quinn brought a group of about twenty people. People loved the food, but by the time we had cleared the last table and closed the doors, we were exhausted. We didn't know how we would possibly have the energy to open the next day. But we did, and then we did it again and again.

That began a period when I worked the hardest in my life, and I've always been a hard worker. Every day, I got up at 7:00 a.m., put on blue jeans, clogs, a white T-shirt, and a coat, walked to work, came home at 10:00 p.m., showered, and fell into bed, dead to the world. We were open every day except Sunday evening. I hardly had time to see my children.

We faced a lot of challenges at the restaurant right away. One month after we opened, in February, there was an enormous storm that buried all of Washington in two feet of snow. People were cross-country skiing down Connecticut Avenue, and word got out that we were open. Suddenly we were slammed, and people didn't want to leave and have to venture back out into the snowstorm. They came at 11:00 a.m. and stayed through dinner, eating and drinking. It was enormous fun in the dining room, but I was in the kitchen working furiously, getting hotter and hotter. I finally realized the snow had smothered our ventilation system. Steven crawled up on the roof and dug it out, and then the party continued.

At first, we could not take a salary, and the only money we lived off came from the tips Thomas got from bartending or hosting. At the end of the week, we'd divide up the big tip jar, and that would pay for our rent and all our expenses.

From the start, we didn't take credit cards, because we couldn't afford to pay the fees. That turned some people off, but others loved it, and it actually worked to our advantage.

We offered to open accounts and bill our guests instead, which they all liked. It functioned like a club: they ran up a tab, and we sent them a monthly bill. That way they became like members of our club, and they kept coming back. Out-of-town guests liked this especially; they'd just send us a check if they didn't have cash. It was honestly pretty naive on our part; by not accepting credit cards, we probably lost a lot of business, especially from expense accounts. We also noted on our menu, posted outside the door, that we were a cash-only business—and so we were held up several times, at gunpoint, for the cash we kept on hand. But we didn't know any better at the time.

I was, however, learning a lot in the kitchen. For one thing, although I'd had great success working with farmers, as a woman I had an altogether different experience when ordering from standard purveyors. I'd talk to the fishmonger, and he'd say, "Hey, babe, because you're so sweet, I'll sell it to you for $6.50 a pound." Then Steven would call and get offered $4.00 a pound right from the start. They thought I was naive and helpless. I couldn't fight that every day, so from then on, Steven took over and ordered all the food. It was unfortunate but true that he seemed to have a lot more buying power as a man.

We were so broke at first that the host and the waiters wrote all the menus by hand every night—thirty a night. Fortunately, that added a homey touch to the restaurant and emphasized the fact that we changed our menu daily. It also meant that the host and the waiters really knew all our dishes by heart.

At first, we could only afford one cook and one dishwasher. Eventually, we were able to hire a baker who did the breads and desserts, as well as an additional cook. I hired a woman named Alison Zaremba, who was a great sous-chef to me for a few years. Alison came from California, and I felt she understood my European sensibility; she had traveled a great deal, and we shared much in common. We used to sit together at the bar, drinking coffee and smoking cigarettes, planning the menu. She introduced me to Mexican-influenced California cuisine—things like guacamole and herbs like cilantro, which expanded my repertoire.

In a few months, we were able to enclose the open patio behind the dining room—the area that was originally where the owners would have kept hay and straw for the horses they used to transport the groceries from the store. We needed more seats, but because the weather in Washington often makes it unpleasant to be outside—whether freezing cold or hot and muggy—we encased the patio in glass and made a garden room. At the same time, we made our bathrooms unisex. I suppose that was a bit unusual back then, too.

I had chosen to call the food at Nora's "additive-free," because there was no real terminology at the time that reflected my style of cooking (though there had been producers of so-called organic foods, it was not until the late 1980s that the term "organic" was recognized and defined by Congress; this was a result of the organic industry's coming together in an attempt to set standards for production and certification). Even though we were soon serving three hundred people a day, and I was using mostly natural foods with no chemical additives, it was still difficult to explain what I was doing. When people read "additive-free," they thought I meant no MSG. Sally Quinn had been right: people didn't come because of the ingredients; they came because they liked the way the food tasted.

In those early years, our menu was eclectic. For appetizers, some of our big hits were Nora's pâté with pickles or smoked trout with horseradish and cucumber salad. At lunch, people loved my curried chicken salad, my roast pork sandwich with cabbage salad, and the roast beef. At dinner, highlights were dishes like beef Stroganoff with noodles, meat loaf with mashed potatoes, steak with potato gratin. There were various pastas—with a Bolognese, carbonara, or puttanesca sauce—that people loved. And lots of chicken dishes—chicken marengo, which is chicken sautéed in garlic and tomatoes, was a big hit too. At the time, pork was the most economical meat for me to use, because, if you're creative, you can use all parts of the pig. So I used the liver for pâté, the ears and jowls for headcheese or terrines, all the trimmings for sausages, the legs for roasts, the shoulder for stew or pork saté. I wasted nothing.

I had contacted all the farmers who had supplied me with local, pesticide-free produce at the Tabard Inn, and of course they were delighted to continue working with me. At the time, many of these farmers were inexperienced; they would pick the vegetables during the day and put them in their trucks, and the vegetables would arrive looking wilted and dead. They had to learn to pick them early in the morning and then keep them cool; also, no one, at that point, had refrigerated trucks. That's one of the reasons that so many health food stores, in their early years, went the way of selling supplements and grains that wouldn't spoil; the produce looked terrible.

I used to take Steven's Buick and get the vegetables locally from the Potomac Vegetable Farms. More farmers began to understand what I needed and started to grow vegetables specifically for the restaurant; I also brought in seeds from Europe so that the farmers would grow what I wanted—arugula, fingerling potatoes, basil, haricots verts, Italian parsley, different varieties of tomatoes. I told the farmers that I would buy everything they grew. Sometimes that meant I'd pay for greens that were full of holes from flea beetles, but I was committed to keeping those farmers in business, and they were committed to growing for me.

Slowly, more "organic" food purveyors were emerging. First, I found the vegetables. Then came the beef, lamb, and veal. I sourced a chicken and duck farmer in Northern California. Then I found more companies, like the New Hampshire–based Stow Mills, that were distributing organic dry goods and other products. Eventually, I found "natural" (hormone- and antibiotic-free) milk, cream, and butter from Lewes Dairy in Delaware or from Mount Ararat in Pennsylvania. Whatever additive-free foods I found dictated what would be on the menu for the given week.

Many of my customers didn't understand the restrictions I was working under. I would get a lot of complaints: "Why don't you have strawberries?" or "Other restaurants have artichokes, why don't you?" I would politely tell them that we liked to serve fruits and vegetables when they were in season and grown nearby and without pesticides, which is how they tasted their very best.

I got so tired of answering those questions that I eventually decided to explain it all on the menu, once we started to photocopy it. The menu read, "New American Food with Additive-Free Ingredients," and a paragraph on the back explained our philosophy—that we felt food should be high in nutrition and also flavor and should be pesticide-free and have no artificial additives. I explained that we feel that local, seasonal food is best, and we try to use it as much as we can. From the start, I listed all my farmers and food sources on the backs of our menus, because I believe people should know where their food is coming from. It read, "We thought you would be interested in knowing where we have found the very special ingredients to prepare the meals which we serve. We feel it is equally important that the people who have worked hard to produce such fine products should be given appropriate credit." Then we went on to list where our beef and pork, veal and lamb, poultry, dairy products, produce, wine, and special Vermont cheddar had been sourced. Today that practice is of course very common, but back then I was certainly one of the first.

The restaurant reviews, initially, were mixed. Like many of the customers, the critics didn't understand my limitations, cooking only with whatever additive-free foods were in season and available. One sniffed, "You only eat carrots and zucchini and everything has dill in it. You're dilled to death at Nora's." It was true; sometimes, the only organic vegetables I could get were carrots and zucchini, and I did use a lot of dill, which married well with the vegetables that were available and gave them a fresh-tasting flavor. But the critics didn't grasp that the whole purpose was to serve food that was part of a delicious, healthy diet, paying attention to the integrity and wholesomeness of the ingredients. I didn't just want to feed people; I wanted to educate them. Other reviewers were kinder: they were enthusiastic about the eclectic menu and the spirit of the restaurant and admired our dedication.

One day, when the critic from the *Washingtonian* came in, one of the servers alerted me that he was there. I was outside, talking to some guests. "Yeah, well, so what?" I replied, and apparently the reviewer overheard me. I was too green to know that I was supposed to give lots of attention and perks to restaurant reviewers, but I'm glad, because it established my policy of not pandering to them. They can enjoy my restaurant and pay for their meal like anyone else. We got a negative review from the *Washingtonian* that time, and I don't believe it gave me a good write-up for the next thirty years.

Still, our reputation spread by word of mouth, and we had a lot of loyal customers. That was thanks, in large part, to the early support of Ben Bradlee. This was at the heyday of *The Washington Post,* a few years after the Watergate exposé written by Bob Woodward and Carl Bernstein led to the resignation of President Richard Nixon. It was a moment when there was a lot of glamour and excitement surrounding journalists—and particularly the *Post*. Ben even covered the 1982 Democratic National Convention using the restaurant telephone and sitting at the bar. He and Sally had a lot of friends, and they brought in a lot of famous people—celebrities, politicians, and journalists. Many years later, Ben reminisced, "Nora's was our neighborhood restaurant. We brought journalists down there. If we had anybody to dinner we did it at Nora's. We sure as hell felt at home there."

Nora's became a hangout for journalists, and a little later it was a magnet for progressives, young diplomats, artists, and celebrities. We never called gossip columnists to brag about our clientele or report on who was stepping out with whom—which a lot of other D.C. restaurants did at the time. As a result, people felt comfortable in our dining room, knowing we wouldn't exploit them. We were discreet—even if it took us a while to figure out that there were some people in Washington you just didn't seat next to others, because of longtime political rivalries or affairs gone sour.

We would be quiet, for example, about overhearing Nora Ephron having a spat at dinner with Carl Bernstein, which she wrote about in a roman à clef, *Heartburn*. Musicians from the Rolling Stones and U2, Sean Penn, Meryl Streep, Diane Keaton, and Lauren Bacall: the list of celebrity diners at Restaurant Nora over the years is a long one. Personally, I was thrilled when Mikhail Baryshnikov came, because I had always loved dancing. The other person who was marvelous was Muhammad Ali. He was a true star; everyone on the staff agreed he was the best celebrity who'd ever walked in. He greeted everyone in the kitchen, posed for photographs, and was incredibly nice. And he had a great smile and kind words for everyone.

Good food, it seems, is also bipartisan. Jimmy Carter was the first president to dine at Nora's. While Restaurant Nora was a haven for Democrats and progressives, Republicans frequented it, too. Nancy Reagan and George Will came often, as did Barry Goldwater. Neither of the Bush presidents ever set foot in Nora's, but Laura Bush came, along with her two daughters.

But for me, the biggest moment was when James Beard came in to visit the restaurant and to meet me.

Beard, along with Elizabeth David, was one of the people whose books had taught me how to cook. He was one of my idols. I loved him because he cooked simple food with seasonal and local American products. He believed we could grow good food and develop a food culture right here. He came from Oregon and used all that wonderful produce they have in the Northwest—apples, cherries, hazelnuts, fish, mushrooms. He was a true inspiration.

Beard wrote a book I loved called *How to Eat Better for Less Money,* which had always been one of my mantras, from my earliest years teaching cooking classes on how to stretch one protein for a week of family dinners. In this book, which was first published in 1954, Beard described how "you, your family and your guests can eat well, often extremely well, at low cost." I liked his tone: "It is not a book for the small and special group who don't have to bother their heads about the cost of food." I also loved the way he defined "gourmet," which he insisted was a much-misunderstood word. "It does not mean rich dishes from the haute cuisine. Actually, the word can be applied to the simplest food—nothing more than a potato cooked to the point at which it bursts its tight skin and shows its snowy interior. It is not the basic cost of the food but the care with which it is selected and prepared that makes it gourmet rather than pedestrian." These sentiments both inspired and encouraged me as I made my own journey into the food world.

Like me, Beard had a fondness for ethnic markets. He knew it often meant a bus or subway ride to an unfamiliar part of town, but he appreciated that not only are the prices generally better, but the produce is often unusual and fresh. You could choose a live chicken in Chinatown and watch as it was killed in front of your eyes—very fresh indeed! But best of all, they have ingredients you could never find anywhere else. "These stores are apt to carry inexpensive foods you may never see in your neighborhood such as stewing fowls, rabbits, pig's feet and hocks, offbeat seafood like squid and eels. And if you like good bread, not the packaged cotton-floss variety, these neighborhoods usually have little bakeries where your bread is freshly baked, honest and good—just like the kind you rave about in Europe."

So it's no wonder that when Beard showed up at Restaurant Nora, it was much more exciting to me than any other celebrity or politician. It was thanks to Bill Rice—executive food editor of *The Washington Post*, who profiled me on the front page of the style section—that Beard visited the restaurant. When Beard arrived, he was in poor health; his gout was so bad that he had to wear slippers. I was gushing over him and taking photographs. He sat there politely as I babbled on about how I like to use the whole animal at my restaurant but was having a hard time selling the liver, kidneys, and tongue.

He was very kind. "They'll eat it. Just prepare it in a flavorful way, make it special, and they'll become familiar with it and will ask for it," he said. "Don't give up."

James Beard gave me the courage to further develop my vision for Nora's. At the time, we were serving a lot of dishes with ground beef, because our small natural farmers couldn't afford to just sell us prime cuts of beef; we had to commit to buy the whole animal and, subsequently, use it all. Further, to raise food in the specific way that I wanted, the farmer had to do it specially for me, so I had a verbal contract with the farmer that I would take a specified amount every week, every month. So I couldn't choose the cut of meat—like twenty New York strip steaks every week—but what I could get was more like a whole cow, every month. The farmer would sell it to me for a low price, but that included the bones and everything, the hanging weight. One animal gave us about seven hundred to nine hundred pounds of meat. Only a quarter of that total would be considered prime cuts—like tenderloin, sirloin, and strip and rib steaks. So I had to learn to be extremely creative about using ground beef. I joked that I should open a chain called the Groundhog, where our entire menu would comprise dishes made from ground meat! But this is when I learned that every culture had recipes made just for these situations—sausages, moussaka, hamburgers, stuffed peppers, pâtés, pasta Bolognese, lasagna, and so on—and so I learned how to make all of them.

My customers, however, continued to request more upscale food—more steak, less meat loaf. They didn't know or care that I had to buy the entire animal from my farmer. We were going to have to come up with some other solution for the ground beef, which would inevitably mean raising our costs so that we could buy more choice cuts. And our costs were already much higher than in most restaurants. Pesticide-free produce costs more than commercial produce—at least 20 percent more—so our margins were very slim, and the volume in the restaurant was exhausting us. At this point, in 1984, I told Steven we needed to upgrade from a neighborhood bistro to a white-tablecloth restaurant. Steven and Thomas agreed. We had already bought out all our original investors and paid back our debts, so it was a good time to take the risk. We wanted to do this ourselves; we wanted to take the gamble. If it worked, we'd make more money; if it didn't, the loss would be ours and only ours.

In 1984, we gathered enough money to take a culinary vacation to consider how to upgrade the restaurant. It was our first vacation in many years, and we finally had a little bit of extra money to eat out and enjoy ourselves. The dollar was very strong, so we were able to visit Michelin-starred restaurants in France and closely examine the menus, wine lists, and presentation.

We started in Paris, where we stayed with Pierre's sister Mireille; Pierre's other sister Monique kindly lent us her car.

I liked them both a lot and always remained in contact with them. From there, we drove to Burgundy. We ate at Bernard Loiseau's restaurant, La Côte d'Or; at L'Espérance in Vézelay; at Maison Lameloise in Chagny; at La Côte Saint Jacques in Joigny. These were experiences like no other.

Of particular importance was our visit to Michel and Christine Guérard's famous Eugénie les Bains, where Guérard has come to be known for his Michelin-starred cuisine, as well as his "slimming" cuisine, for which he had earned three Michelin stars by 1977. We had the great privilege of visiting the Guérards' gardens on the Eugénie property. This was the first time I had ever tasted purslane, which I ate straight from the ground and then later tasted again when Michel served it as a salad.

We visited farms and wineries as often as possible, including a foie gras farm. When I saw how the ducks were force-fed and learned how foie gras was made, I decided right then and there that I could live without foie gras. And to this day, I never serve it at my restaurant.

One afternoon, while driving through the French countryside, we encountered a farm where we were able to buy a just-killed chicken and have it prepared for us. It was simply roasted, with a little oil, herbs, salt, and pepper. We took it with us, bought a baguette and a bottle of Cahors, the local red wine, and had a picnic. We couldn't believe how delicious everything was; we ate it with our fingers and marveled at its incredible simplicity and flavor.

In France, they are very particular about the china and

crystal, as well as the design of the menu, the decor, and the service. I was especially struck by the wonderful service—the ceremonial lifting of the cloche from a dish, a tasting menu with six or seven courses. I was not used to this very rich food—the many courses. At a certain point, I had to stop eating, but in each instance we didn't want to insult the chef, so often Steven was eating my food as well as his! I was impressed by the beauty of the food—a piece of protein with a perfect sauce, a few delicately placed vegetables: a baby carrot, perfectly cooked; a crispy potato galette. But I was surprised that the emphasis was more about the overall effect—the service, the decor, the flavor, and the beauty of the finished dish.

When we returned, we were inspired. Before, I hadn't given much thought to which vegetables went with which dish, so the meat loaf and the salmon, for example, both came with the same vegetables. Now I knew that I wanted to make each vegetable specific to the dish at hand. I also wanted to use the inspiration of French service and attention to detail at Nora's—to make each diner feel that his or her meal was a special experience—only, in my version, with organic food.

So we redecorated, taking out several tables so people would feel they had more privacy while dining and adding a few larger tables for bigger parties. We bought new white porcelain dishes, as well as weightier silverware and glassware. We threw away the calico tablecloths, which had gotten ratty from so many washings, and replaced them with cream-colored linens. We took down the poster-sized photographs and traveled to Pennsylvania to find some Americana art and artifacts. I continued to want my cuisine to be viewed as representing the multiethnic melting pot that is the United States, but I wanted to slightly change the approach to make the restaurant more upscale and more special.

Next, I rewrote the menu, using better cuts of meat, changing from ground meat and stews to grilled and sautéed items—from secondary cuts to prime cuts. I realized that I needed another outlet for our secondary cuts of meats, so I found a local school where our farmer could sell some of our ground beef; this way, we didn't have to worry about using it all up. We added different vegetables, which I asked my farmers to grow just for me—lots of new leaf lettuces, spinach, different varieties of tomatoes, and so on. We retrained the servers and repainted, and when we opened, we had a lovely fine-dining establishment.

We had to double our prices.

Our regulars were furious, particularly the journalists at the *Post,* who didn't get paid huge salaries and had been our core supporters. They were worried that they'd lost their home—their clubhouse. We were terrified at first, thinking the new Restaurant Nora would be a failure. Thomas fretted that our expensive upgrade would ruin us. I lay awake at night, worrying that we'd lose everything we'd worked so hard to build.

As a response to the backlash, we came up with an idea to help win back our loyal customers. We decided to invite all our clients who had personal accounts with us—the ones we'd billed over the years, from the time when we didn't take credit cards. For two nights, we set up a big buffet in the middle of the restaurant, and they were our guests, wining and dining for free. We concentrated on roasts and steaks, along with an array of vegetables and salads, as well as a wide selection of cheeses and desserts. We served everything from the new menu, and people loved it.

We won back most of our old customers, even if many of them came less frequently. We attracted new customers, too, because when we reopened, we were reviewed more widely than we had ever been before. The reviews were generally good, but I was surprised that once again none of the critics acknowledged that we were serving organic food.

We'd become much stricter about our sourcing, preferring certified organic to "natural," which was always a fuzzy label. The back of the new menu said that we tried to find the most organically raised and grown food that we could, food without any chemical additives, such as pesticides, growth-promoting hormones, or antibiotics. We sourced them both locally and nationally, which was easier now that there were several organic and natural food distributors. I suppose I wanted reviewers to take note of what made us unique, the mission statement behind the food we were serving on the plates. But that would come later.

In the end, our transition to fine dining worked for us. We made the same amount of money serving 150 people instead of 300, which made the pace less frantic and the quality and the presentation of the food much better.

. . .

Over the next couple years, we would continue to make improvements in the restaurant. In order to do that, we needed to buy the building outright. In 1986, we contacted the owners, three sisters, none of whom lived in Washington, and after much negotiation they sold the building to us. At that point, we were able to make big structural changes. We took out the acoustical ceiling to expose the rafters and installed better carpet. We built a new bar and put in marble tiles for the floor, and extensively remodeled the kitchen.

When we first went looking for decorative art in Pennsylvania, I'd fallen in love with Amish crib quilts. We put out the word that we were interested in these quilts to some "pickers" who went among Amish families to see who had crib quilts to sell. We ended up with a beautiful collection, which we preserve carefully; these days, the Textile Museum in D.C. takes a tour to the restaurant to show off our museum-quality art.

CHAPTER 8

City Café and Asia Nora

By the mid-1980s I wasn't satisfied to leave things as they were. I had decided that I wanted to expand my vision of Nora's into something bigger—a place that addressed a healthy lifestyle. Inspired, perhaps, by my earlier visit to Eugénie les Bains, I wanted to create a place where people could spend time in nature—bicycling, hiking, playing tennis—and enjoy delicious healthy cuisine. I hoped to create it at a hot spring; not only would it be healthy to soak in the mineral baths, and drink the water, but the hot water from the spring could heat greenhouses to grow organic food year-round. Our guests could immerse themselves in a relaxing environment and go away inspired.

Steven and I had been on the lookout for a place to build this sort of getaway for a couple of years. We had taken trips whenever we could to check out hot springs in Colorado, Nevada, Washington State, Idaho, and Northern California.

Each one we found had some problem: the springs weren't hot enough, access was difficult, the price was out of reach. Finally, we found a place near Soledad, California, called Paraiso Hot Springs. Other than the fact that it was near a prison, it was perfect. The property had two hundred acres, surrounded by vineyards and agricultural land, and the Ventana Wilderness with the Santa Lucia Mountains was nearby for hiking.

By then, I had befriended Andrew Weil, the physician who has always been far ahead of his time in understanding and promoting alternative medicine. We had a very similar perspective about health, and Andrew agreed to come on board for our spa. He would do the mind/health concept, I would do the food, and Steven would manage the whole place. It was going to be a big step; it would mean leaving Washington, at least part-time, and completely uprooting our lives. But we were ready for the change and the challenge.

To our great dismay, however, our offer did not go through; the owners later sold the property to a developer who turned it into a golf course. I was very disappointed that there would be no California spa and wellness resort. It was my dream to create such a place, and with Andrew it would have been perfect.

We decided to keep looking, but closer to home. Near Olney, in Maryland on the outskirts of Washington, we found a tavern with a beautiful old barn that I thought we could convert into a yoga studio and a place where we could cater events, but it meant driving through strip malls to get there, which destroyed its charm. We found another place in Virginia that was an old horse estate, but it was expensive and needed a lot of work. We were beginning to get discouraged.

Still, Steven kept reading the real estate ads. One day, he came across an announcement for the auction of a country club with a golf course on the Shenandoah River. It sounded great—near Washington, in the country, and on a scenic river. I was imagining replacing the golfing green with hiking trails and bicycle paths, as well as gardens so that guests could see where the vegetables for their dinner grew before eating from our spa menu.

Steven called me from the auction.

"I'm the only one here," he said, almost gleeful. "This country club is for sale. It's 150 acres right on the river—for 200,000. What should I do?"

"Buy it!" I told him. And so we found ourselves the owners of a country club and golf course on the Shenandoah River in Virginia.

The next weekend, Steven, Thomas, their sister Marguerite, and I drove out to see the property. It was lovely country, with a wide, grassy area along the river where the golf course currently sat and a low-slung clubhouse that abutted the hills, which we thought we could turn into the restaurant. We'd brought along a picnic lunch to enjoy on our new land. But the moment we sat down, we were surrounded by swarms of gnats. We tried to swat them away but to no avail. By the end of the day, we had to take refuge inside the clubhouse. It didn't take long to realize that of the 150 acres we'd rather impulsively bought, 120 were on a floodplain, which was a breeding ground for insects. The ground was moist, and there were clouds of little gnats everywhere that drove you berserk. The only way to get rid of them, it turned out, was to spray pesticide, which is what the former owners usually did. We'd bought pesticide-laden land. This wasn't going to work.

"We just need to find some organic mosquito repellent," I said. I was also thinking about the birdhouses that the Amish use; the starlings keep the mosquitoes and other insect popu-lations down. "Maybe it won't be so bad."

It was a short-lived euphoria, then, being landowners of a piece of property on the Shenandoah River. For a couple of months, we considered our options. Fortunately, a realtor approached us and said a client wanted to buy the country club. We decided to sell, aside from ten acres on top of a ridge that were fairly distant from the floodplain. Maybe, I thought, we could still do something with that. Steven agreed, and we sold the country club, aside from that small bit of property, at a good profit, so we were relieved. I abandoned my dream of a spa and focused instead on things closer to home.

By this point, it was 1985, a year that brought some difficult changes in my personal life. Pierre and I had remained friendly, and we did a good job of co-parenting, even though our lives were separate. I felt, on some level, that he was a soul mate, whether or not I was with Steven. Pierre had told me regularly, since we separated, that we could get back together. I never believed we would, but regardless of the changes that happen with marriage and divorce, there are some people with whom you will always have a connection, a relationship for life. That's how it was with Pierre. To that end, we never divorced; we had agreed not to do so, unless one of us asked for it. Our children had asked this of us, and we had said we would remain married. We respected each other, and we agreed that if the other person wanted to remarry, that would be fine, we would not object, but until then we would remain legally married. We had a legal separation document, to keep Pierre from being responsible for any business debts, but that was it. The boys had always lived with Pierre, Pierre had no financial responsibility toward me, and the only thing I would receive was money from the sale of the house, should he ever choose to sell it.

But now Pierre had met a Canadian woman nearly half his age—he was, at this point, sixty—and in 1985 she gave birth to their daughter, Veronique. Suddenly Pierre had a new family. He made it clear that I would not be able to count on him in the ways that I had in the past. This, in turn, forced me to realize that our life together was officially finished—that our children remained the only real link, even though they too were getting older.

For the most part, my sons had not lived with me during their childhood, but I had been responsible for their education, and we lived on the same street, so the boys were in and out of my house all the time. Steven did not want to be their father, as they already had Pierre, so my life with Steven functioned separately. It was an unorthodox structure, especially for the time, but it worked for all of us. Now, however, Alexis was getting ready to graduate from high school, and Olivier was nearly there.

In October of that year, for my birthday, as always, I received a call from my sister Rosi. I had not seen Rosi for almost a year, when I'd last visited her to go skiing in Austria. Because of travel restrictions involved with getting a green card, not to mention my intense work schedule, it had been difficult to go to Europe to visit my family as often as I would have liked. I was working when Rosi called that day and didn't get back to her right away.

Since my move to the United States, it was difficult to stay in close contact. It was just too expensive and logistically complicated to visit often, though I tried my best to get to Austria once every two years. (Later I could manage twice a year—once in the winter and once in the summer—especially when my parents got older.) We stayed in contact, of course, but telephone calls were expensive and letters took a long time. There was no e-mail or Skype, so we were dependent on these visits to catch up with each other. It was much harder for them to come to visit me; my mother came three times, twice for the births of my sons and then once for a visit. Both Rosi and Christa came only once. Christa, in particular, was shocked when she came; she couldn't get over our small apartment or how much I worked. My life was very different from the life she was leading at home.

A week after my birthday, and my missed call from Rosi,

my sister Christa called me in tears, crying, telling me that Rosi had taken her own life.

I was stunned, shocked, and feeling guilty. I knew that Rosi had rarely been happy since the time we were girls, skiing together. She'd suffered from manic depression for years and had experienced a series of difficulties and setbacks that had finally sunk into what had seemed a relentless depression. I felt terribly guilty that I hadn't made enough of an effort to visit her and support her and that she had called me when she was likely desperate and depressed and I wasn't there for her.

The only good thing to come from Rosi's death was that it brought me closer to Christa. I realized how precious it was to have a sister, and I vowed that we would talk more and spend more time together. I didn't ever want to feel guilty about our relationship.

That was a very dark November. Once again, I threw myself into my work. Restaurant Nora, though successful, was still struggling with our meat problem. The more prime cuts we wanted to serve, the more we still had to deal with an excess of ground beef. There was only so much that the school I'd found would take, and I didn't want to change my supplier, Mr. Garnett, from whom I'd bought for years and whose ethos and values were important to me.

Right around this time, we got a call from the developer who had bought the country club from us. He felt he needed the other acres we had kept on the ridge to make his property work. We chose to sell him the land, which gave us sufficient funds to invest in a new restaurant. Our plan was to make it a simple café or bistro, where we could serve dishes like burgers and stews that would use the secondary cuts of meat we couldn't use at Restaurant Nora. Hopefully, this would solve the meat problem!

Once again, Steven and I started looking at property for a restaurant. Steven found a building in the West End section of Washington, on M Street. It had been the Population Reference Bureau, built by David Schwarz, a famous D.C. architect. It was an up-and-coming neighborhood at the time, with new trees, hotels, and the promise of its becoming a gateway from downtown to Georgetown. The building, which was three stories, was expensive, but we liked the space. Steven and Thomas told me that this building would be a great investment—our life insurance, which we could sell for many times what we paid for it in a few years. We found some additional investors, bought the building, and started planning our new restaurant.

Our architect, David Schwarz, remodeled the building into a modern space, turning the first two floors of the town house into a restaurant. We decided to call it City Café. I loved how it looked. Schwarz had made a triangular opening between the first and the second floors and put mirrors on the walls so that it looked as if there were a big square opening, which made the place seem much bigger. The triangular motif was repeated all over the place, with triangular tables and lots of molding. The color scheme was all different shades of pink, from beige to true rose, with black chairs and black faux-marble tabletops. It had an entirely different feel from Restaurant Nora; it was sleek and modern.

When we opened City Café, we closed our lunch service at Nora's. Lunch had never been a brisk business for us. The restaurant is in a residential section near Dupont Circle where there are no other commercial buildings. City Café would go on to have a much better lunch business, with professionals from law firms and tourists from nearby hotels. We found tenants for the upstairs office spaces, which helped pay for the expensive building.

One of my chefs from Restaurant Nora, Steve Pickell, became the chef at City Café. He was very good, a Californian who brought a light touch to the food. He expanded my menu with an excellent rotisserie chicken and found all sorts of ways to use our ground beef: tacos, quesadillas, stuffed peppers, hamburgers, and pâtés. We changed the menu not every day but seasonally. Of course, we still used organic produce for everything. Steven ran this restaurant, not me—which was good, because by then I was nine months pregnant.

Yes, that's right: I was forty-four years old and nine months pregnant.

For some time, Steven and I had talked about having a child together. We'd had our ups and downs over the previous few years, and this topic was a part of the trouble. I knew, once I turned forty, that if this was something we wanted, I didn't have much time left, but Steven insisted on waiting. We even separated for a time, which was really painful for me. Steven moved to the apartment above the restaurant for three or four months. But we decided to stick it out—we realized that we really did love each other—so he came home, and we began talking about having a child in earnest.

It wasn't an easy process. One doctor told me I was in menopause already; a fertility specialist was similarly unhelpful, even cruel, blaming—inaccurately, as we now know—my inability to get pregnant on my hectic lifestyle, not my age. It was a very discouraging time.

I decided to take things into my own hands. First, I saw a naturopath, who told me I should stop smoking and drinking coffee and wine; in his opinion, I was bombarding myself with stimulants. I stopped coffee and only drank a little wine with meals. Then I went to see a Korean acupuncturist, who took my pulses and suggested regular acupuncture sessions.

"You're too skinny. You need to put on some weight," he said. It was true: I was working so hard I had very little body fat.

I had several weeks of treatments, and then Steven and I went on vacation. If stress was part of the problem, we would unwind a little. We traveled to California, to check out restaurants and to visit Alexis, who was, at this point, living in Oakland. We took a slow drive down the coast along Route 1, stopping to see friends along the way who lived in Big Sur. We also wanted to check out brewpubs in California; they were just coming in style, and we were considering opening a microbrewery in D.C. We had a wonderful time, wandering around San Francisco and Los Angeles, exploring neighbor-hoods and brewpubs, trying new restaurants. We were able to forget any problems with the restaurant and getting pregnant and just relax. When I got home, I was pregnant.

I know this isn't the case for all women; it is essential, today, that we have a good understanding of the science of fertility and all the many options available to us. I know that many women struggle for years to get pregnant, no matter what alternative or traditional routes they try. I also know I was lucky—that even at forty-three, I was eventually able to get pregnant naturally. I am very grateful for that and for whatever prompted it, even today.

On February 14, I was working in the kitchen at Restaurant Nora—Valentine's Day is always busy at any restaurant—and had tired myself out, as I was due at any moment. The next day, Sunday, we relaxed and went to a movie. That evening, my water broke. I knew I had some time before the baby came, so I didn't go see the doctor until Monday. I suppose I was a little casual about it, but after all I'd delivered Olivier by myself!

Although I had wanted to give birth at home, my doctor advised against it, because of my age. Our daughter, Nina—whom we named after my great friend Nina Sutton—was born around 10:00 p.m. Nina was a wonderful baby and, compared with Alexis and Olivier, extremely easy. She slept and nursed very well. I wanted to stay at home with her for a long time, but after a couple of weeks—a very short time—Steven asked me to go back to work. He said I had to be there. I don't know why

I agreed to it, but I did. Carmen, a woman who used to work for us in the restaurant, wanted to take care of Nina; she came to the house every morning around 9:00, and I went to work until the evening.

Still, from the beginning, I tried to take Nina with us whenever possible. I would put her in a little woven basket, a *moïse*, like those you use at the market in France, and travel with her everywhere. We went to California with her in her basket and then later took her to Europe, where we'd bring her along to restaurants. We would ask for a corner seat and put her on the floor, and she would sleep while we had a leisurely dinner. She was such a good baby that people didn't mind.

A few years after Nina was born, Steven and I decided we wanted to have another child. But I was in my late forties. I had three children already and was quite content, but Steven desperately wanted to adopt, and so I agreed. Through a friend, he met a Russian woman from Irkutsk who lived in D.C. and ran an adoption agency from Siberia. This was after perestroika, when the state no longer supported many orphanages, which were then left to fend for themselves. As a result, the orphanages opened their doors to foreign adoptions.

By then, Nina was nearly six years old, and Steven didn't want to have a newborn. He felt there would be too much difference in age for them to become friends. He wanted to adopt a child who was at least two or three years old. We spent a long time talking with the woman at the adoption agency and went through the process of being checked out by a social worker. She told me I was too old to adopt a child and frowned upon the fact that Steven and I were not married. So, because Steven was still in his thirties, we decided that he would adopt the child by himself, as a single parent.

Eventually, the adoption agency found a girl for us. Steven, Nina, and I traveled to Irkutsk to meet Nadia at the orphanage. It was arranged that we would spend a week there to see if this felt like the right fit for our family.

The trip was surreal. We flew to Moscow from Vienna laden with many suitcases, because they had asked us to bring a lot of presents and things like tampons, underwear, and sneakers that were, at the time, considered luxuries in Russia. From Moscow, we took a ten-hour flight to Irkutsk, which was nothing like a U.S. flight. There were no flight attendants to tell people to buckle up; passengers were standing in the aisles, some drinking vodka straight out of a bottle, while we were taking off and landing. After six hours, we refueled in Omsk, where the bathrooms were rudimentary and there was nothing to eat. Back on the plane, Pekingese dogs ran up and down the aisles, on their way to be sold in Mongolia; chickens in cages were stacked at the back of the plane. We couldn't use the one bathroom for the entire flight, because someone had vomited, passed out, and blocked the door. Needless to say, we were relieved to arrive.

Irkutsk is a small Mongolian town, with wooden houses, each with a different window treatment carved out of wood. At the time, it was quite poor, with very little infrastructure or support. Many houses were missing windows, and garbage was everywhere. We found no restaurants where we could eat—except what were the equivalent of private social clubs. The director of the orphanage invited us to one of these clubs to dine on smoked salmon, caviar, vodka, and champagne. The next day, we went to see Nadia in the orphanage. She was three years old and tiny; her hair was wispy and blond, though there wasn't much of it. The orphanage had outfitted her with an enormous bow on top of her head. Initially, she was not very responsive to us: she could not look us in the eye and was uncommunicative. Given the situation in the orphanage, we weren't surprised. There were perhaps fifteen children with one adult to supervise. There were big cribs with four babies in each one, all without diapers, lying in their own urine. Many of the kids had hepatitis. At meals, the children ate bowls of gruel, along with a couple slices of cucumber and salami, with only water to drink. They were silent. None of the children had their own clothes; they just put on whatever was clean. They didn't have toys, either; I gave the people who ran the orphanage some money to buy toys, but they told me they would just get broken.

We took Nadia out to the playground and asked if we could take her back with us that night. We wanted to try to connect with her. But Nina was already certain. "You know, Mommy and Daddy, once we bring her to America, everything will be okay," she told us. "She will be okay."

That was all we needed to make a decision. When we told the director of the orphanage, he was elated. Nadia had been difficult to place because of her age; she had also been a sickly child from a difficult background. Her early years had been tough.

My heart went out to this little girl; I wanted to bring her home, feed her some good food, and make her healthy.

We knew it wouldn't be easy to raise this wounded child. At first, we couldn't even communicate; we didn't speak a common language, of course. She basically didn't speak at all. Eating was also a problem. She would put a piece of bread in her mouth and suck on it, rather than chewing, as if to make it last longer. When she saw butter, she took the whole stick and ate it straight. I think her body was craving fat. A nutritionist explained that babies in these orphanages are often given formula diluted with tea and don't get enough fat and vitamins. But being essentially raised in a healthy restaurant helped Nadia to quickly overcome any nutritional difficulties.

In the early 1990s, the hectic nature of my personal life given my two new young children was easily matched by the way my restaurants were growing and changing. By 1992, Restaurant Nora was becoming more and more of a destination for politicians. When Bill Clinton was elected, we knew the restaurant would become a hangout for his administration. We decided we would transform the upstairs apartment at the restaurant, where we had offices, into a private dining room. We wanted the room to be ready for the inauguration.

We asked David Schwarz to design the new space. We

combined two rooms to make one big dining room for special events and changed a small bedroom into my office. Soon, we bought the building next door and turned that into another private dining room—the Wine Library—and put offices in upstairs. Finally, we were humming along as a business: I had an office, and so did Steven and Thomas and the special events director.

We were delighted to be able to open the upstairs dining room for an inaugural party for President Clinton. He was always wonderful in the restaurant, he worked the room effortlessly, and I marveled at how he remembered the names of so many people. He was nice to the staff, too, and treated them with the same kind of respect as the important guests in the dining room. I admired that about him. As a result, Restaurant Nora continued to do well; it became an unofficial dining room of the Clinton administration, and evenings were busy. City Café, unfortunately, was starting to slow down. Many of the firms around us had installed cafeterias in their buildings, so fewer people came to lunch at our restaurant. There was also a downturn in the economy, which affected our business. What had once been a standard of three-martini lunches over several courses turned into a little salad with a glass of iced tea and "Please, can I have a refill and the check?" Dinner reservations dropped too. With the recession in the 1990s, fewer people were staying at hotels, especially the ones in the neighborhood, as they were all quite upscale. City Café had had a good run, but it was starting to become clear to us that its time was over.

Steven, Thomas, and I discussed what to do next. I thought we should simply open a bar: the area was busy with young workers who wanted a place to sit and hang out over a cocktail before going home. I wanted to make the downstairs an enormous bar with a couple of high tables, places to mingle, music, maybe even dancing. If people wanted to have a more substantial meal, they could eat upstairs. But Steven didn't want to get into the headaches that he felt a bar would entail, dealing with drunk and rowdy people.

My next idea was an upscale vegetarian restaurant. As part of my quest to bring an even healthier diet to my restaurants, I was beginning to de-emphasize meat. I believed then, and still do now, that in the healthiest diets meat was not the star but more of a condiment, eaten occasionally, not necessarily every meal or every day, and certainly not in large quantities.

Steven and Thomas voted down the vegetarian restaurant, saying that Washington wasn't ready for it. I disagreed; after all, this was when Charlie Trotter was successfully doing a hundred-dollar vegetarian tasting menu in Chicago. Then I proposed another idea—why not try opening an Asian-inspired restaurant but using local and organic produce as we did in our current venues? I was curious to see if I could make pan-Asian food more accessible to the American palate. I wanted to use Asian ingredients that brought freshness and spice to the plate—ginger, lemongrass, tamarind, cilantro, curry, mint, Thai basil, and chilies—but use techniques that were more Western. My partners agreed this seemed appealing, so we began to plan Asia Nora.

I went to New York City to eat at a lot of Asian restaurants and to take cooking classes with cookbook authors and other chefs to learn about Vietnamese, Thai, Chinese, and Indian cooking. Every day had a whole-day class with a different teacher. It had been a long time since my Chinese cooking class when I first moved to the United States! It was fun for me to take these classes and experiment with such wonderful ingredients, thinking about how to incorporate them into my menu.

That summer, I went to Nevada to visit my old friend Maya Miller on her ranch. It's a wonderful place: the house has a main room with a big kitchen that spills into the living room, surrounded by floor-to-ceiling windows, with a view of the wide-open prairie. The ranch sits up next to the eastern Sierras, where I could go hiking in the mornings. Maya always had many friends passing through; even though she lived in rural Nevada, there were all sorts of interesting people who came, and everyone ate dinner together. The ranch also had an organic garden filled with many vegetables and herbs.

I brought along a suitcase full of Asian ingredients, which are difficult to find in Reno, and then I began to cook. Each day, I experimented with different recipes from all over South and Southeast Asia. One evening it would be Indian, the next evening Thai. I played with the recipes I had, modifying them for an American palate by omitting some of the extreme flavorings, like fermented shrimp paste or dried shrimp, too much hot pepper or chili paste. At dinner, people would tell me which dishes they liked best and which they would order at a restaurant. It was a lot of fun to experiment with all these dishes in a relaxed, beautiful atmosphere. And as usual, it made me feel great to cook for friends who appreciated fresh, flavorful meals.

Before I left Washington, I'd searched all over D.C. and Virginia for different handicrafts we could use for the decor. That was really fun; though I had never become an interior designer, I still loved decorating and using my eye for color, craft, and atmosphere. I bought all kinds of masks, kimonos, paintings, and pieces of furniture. I found an interior decorator for the restaurant and left the art and the café in his hands. The decorator had spent many years in Thailand, so he was perfect for the job of transforming the City Café into our vision for Asia Nora. We chose to call it Asia Nora to tie it to our original restaurant, in order to benefit from the connection and to explain our consistent philosophy of using natural and organic ingredients.

When I got home, Steven brought me straight from the airport to the new restaurant. I couldn't believe it was the same space. Our designer had turned a casual bistro into a gorgeous, sophisticated restaurant. He took the Japanese obis, which are traditional ceremonial ties that go around the waist, and used them to make valances for the windows. He made little collages with all different types of hats to hang on the walls, as well as hanging shrimp traps. All the pink wood trim that had been everywhere was now painted in faux mahogany, and mahogany tabletops were installed to match. We kept the same chairs but made slipcovers from an embroidered shiny, silky material. All of our china was made by a woman in her seventies who was a great potter; she made more than one hundred square plates, each with a different design. Some were celadon green, some oxblood red. The chopstick holders were Balinese green stones that my son Olivier introduced me to (by this time, Olivier had moved to Bali, where he still lives). The atmosphere was very special. I adored it. At first, it was difficult to find a chef who was willing to marry traditional techniques with a lighter style of cooking and nontraditional, slightly Americanized spicing and flavoring. After trying several chefs, none of whom were the right fit, I was introduced to Yuriko Matsuura, a Japanese woman who came as an intern from L'Academie de Cuisine in Maryland. She did a six-month internship at Asia Nora; she later came to Restaurant Nora as a sous-chef for two years. To this day, she remains a close friend and comes to work at Restaurant Nora six months out of every year, during which time she stays with me. At the time, however, she did something quite brave for a young student: she gathered up her courage to tell Steven and me that the current chef was treating everyone very poorly and that after six months she couldn't wait to get out of what was a terrible situation. He was a very good cook, but I knew he could never build up a team, and that was not how I wanted my kitchen run or my employees treated.

Yuriko went back to school to finish, and I decided to turn my attention west, to San Francisco, where I thought I might find a chef who understood the culinary balance I was searching for. I went to the Bay Area to interview various chefs. That's where I found Christian Thornton. I visited Christian on the boat where he lived, and he cooked for me from his tiny kitchen. He had prepared a very simple, perfect tomato salad, with excellent olive oil, along with a piece of poached salmon with a gingery relish. Over lunch, he told me that he wanted to move to the East Coast because his girlfriend and child were living in Virginia, which meant, to me, that he would stay at the restaurant for a long time. So I hired him, and he went on to do a great job at Asia Nora. He developed a strong team, was a good teacher, and was also a very social person and went out into the dining room to talk with customers. He developed a great menu, and people loved to go there.

The critical reception, initially, was mixed. Phyllis Richman of *The Washington Post* called it "fusion confusion" and said she didn't know why she should go to Asia Nora for a dish that wasn't authentic when she could have a real dish around the corner for $5.95 at a Chinese restaurant. But she missed what I was trying to do. Nobody mentioned that I used produce from local farmers, either. It wasn't entirely organic, because I had too many Asian ingredients that were impossible to source as organics, but it was close. Today I see restaurants using fresh, local, and organic produce and meats and think, *I did that first!* But at the time, the mission behind the restaurant wasn't entirely understood.

Still, people came and continued to come. I really trusted Christian—he was a great chef—so I didn't spend a lot of time at Asia Nora, except to eat there, with pleasure, once or twice a week, so that I could taste the food and make sure they continued to use local and organic ingredients. I was happy the restaurant was in good hands. Even when Christian left a few years later, things kept up well; Haidar Karoum, a Lebanese Irish chef who was then the sous-chef at Restaurant Nora, took over, and he ran things incredibly well until 2007, when he had the opportunity to open his own restaurant, Proof, where today he remains the executive chef and partner and continues to source from local producers as much as possible.

Late in the first decade of the twenty-first century, real estate values around Asia Nora, in the West End, jumped up again. A real estate developer bought the Nigerian embassy building, which was next door, and he wanted to buy our building, too, so that he could combine the lots and build a new hotel with a garage. Ultimately, after much negotiation, we were able to get a very favorable deal for the building. It felt like the right thing and gave me some money to put away for retirement. That said, diners in D.C. were less happy; I still get complaints from people who lament that Asia Nora is gone.

When Asia Nora closed, it created an opportunity for me to do more than run restaurants. I had become more and more passionate about the organic food movement, and it was time for me to put my energy into taking my message out of the dining room and into the world.

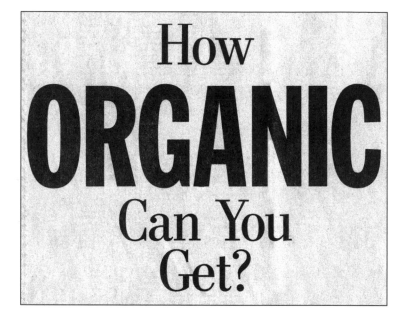

CHAPTER 9

The First Certified Organic Restaurant

By the late 1980s, Americans had started to take notice of organic foods. The circulation of *Organic Gardening* magazine grew from 260,000 in the 1960s to over 1.5 million in the 1980s. Whole Foods Market opened in Austin, Texas, with a staff of nineteen. The Organic Trade Association, which represents organic producers, farmers, and distributors, formed in 1985. In 1986, outraged at the opening of a McDonald's near the Spanish Steps in Rome, Carlo Petrini started the slow-food movement, striving to preserve traditional and regional foods and promoting a way of life that opposes the fast-food culture. Organics got a lot of publicity in 1989, when CBS's *60 Minutes* aired "Intolerable Risk: Pesticides in Our Children's Food," highlighting a report by the Natural Resources Defense Council on the carcinogenic risks of the chemical Alar (daminozide), a growth regulator sprayed on apples; Meryl Streep appeared on the *Donahue* show to support local farms and organic foods, which caused a public outcry. All of that served to wake people up about the importance of organic foods. People who came to my restaurant for the dining experience were realizing that I was onto something with my insistence on organic foods, and they began to read the back of the menu more, where I sourced my ingredients, and asked me a lot more questions about farmers and how the produce and meat were raised.

But there was still a great deal of confusion about what was "natural," "organic," or "healthy." Several states had passed standards for organic certification, but in other states the term "organic" was thrown around loosely, for marketing purposes, as vague and ultimately meaningless as the term "green." The U.S. government needed to develop standards so that people could understand just what it was that they were eating— foods grown without pesticides, fungicides, or other unhealthy chemicals, using traditional farming methods, like composting and rotating diverse crops, that keep the soil healthy.

Finally, in 1990, after a great deal of work by many advocates, the U.S. government passed a regulation, as part of the Food, Agriculture, Conservation, and Trade Act, that called for the creation of nationwide standards for organic certification, which I had supported. I was honored to speak when the bill passed as an example of the promise of what an organic future could look like. I spoke from the steps of the Cannon House Office Building on Pennsylvania Avenue, where Senator Patrick Leahy of Vermont had asked me to say a few words about the importance of the regulations. While the national standards ultimately took nearly ten years to accomplish, the 1990 act was the first step. Three years later, the European Union established a common definition for "organic," creating a phenomenal growth in organics there. This, too, was very exciting for me. Only with specific standards for what "organic" means can consumers understand and trust the labels on their food.

I could see that there was real momentum building in the realm of organic foods. My restaurants were running smoothly, and I started to crave a new challenge. At this point, Restaurant Nora had been open for more than a decade, and I wanted to do something bigger. With the government involved, this was becoming a national movement—one that was much bigger, and more powerful, than the grassroots movement of two restaurants that I had going myself. So I began to attend conferences and become involved in organizations that were promoting healthy foods and a cleaner environment on a broader level.

In the early 1990s, I went to Nuremberg, Germany, to attend the BIOFACH convention, the largest organic show in the world. It was inspiring; an enormous convention complex was filled with products and representatives from only organic businesses. Everything was organic—wine, clothing, furniture, sausage, bread, cookies, drinks—from countries all around the world, including Italy, Greece, Germany, Turkey, and Austria. Europe was developing a strong organic movement and had already established government regulations and organic standards; I wanted to be part of bringing that to America. There was already a natural foods expo in the United States, with just a small organic section, mainly food, but the BIOFACH expo comprised everything and was incredibly impressive to me for its sheer scale and diversity of products.

Around the same time, a Japanese cookbook publisher visited Restaurant Nora and was impressed by what we were doing. He asked me to write a cookbook that emphasized organic, seasonal food, in an attempt to encourage small organic farmers in Japan so they could see that there was a market for it. I liked this idea, and so I did it. The book went on to be published in Japan in 1994.

I also joined the board of a consumer advocacy group called Public Voice for Food and Health Policy. While at a board meeting in New York, some of us went to visit the Union Square farmers' market. I was flabbergasted; here were farmers from all over the region selling beautiful produce—tomatoes, peaches, gorgeous heads of lettuce, eggplants of all shapes and sizes and shades of purple—to New Yorkers. There were cheeses and meats and breads and cakes. People wandered around, tasting samples, chatting with those who had grown or made the food. Several of the farmers were small organic producers. It was a Saturday scene that everyone seemed to love.

I immediately knew that I had to try to organize a farmers' market back home in Washington, D.C. While there had always been one small market at Eastern Market on Capitol Hill, it was not a producer-only farmers' market. I discussed the idea with the executive director of Public Voice for Food and Health Policy, and he told me that if I could organize the logistics, he could get me the seed money to make it happen.

I knew I didn't have time to organize it myself, but I knew the perfect candidate: my friend Ann Yonkers, a fellow member of Les Dames d'Escoffier, an international philanthropic society of women food professionals. She had been a great help as my co-writer when I'd published my cookbook, *Cooking with Nora*, a few years earlier, and she understood the importance of supporting small organic farmers, a cause for which she was an advocate. She took some convincing, but soon she flew into action, researching sites and forming alliances with local producers. It took about two years to open the first market at Dupont Circle. Many businesses and neighborhoods in Washington hadn't wanted to bring farmers in. They were so disconnected from their food and land that they thought the farmers would just be tracking in mud from the country, creating a mess. It was very difficult to get a permit and to get the neighborhood association on board, as well as the neighbors. We had several meetings with community groups to convince them that the market would be a wonderful asset to Washington, explaining how much farmers' markets had revitalized other cities. We also had to persuade a local bank to let us use its parking lot on Sunday, which it resisted until it realized it was a cash business and it would make a lot of money from ATM fees.

Ann developed a relationship with people from the American Farmland Trust, who said they would support the market and serve as the nonprofit umbrella. Finally, the Dupont Circle farmers' market opened in 1997. Today, it's bigger than ever, helping sustain a lot of local farmers. It's great for the community: it's like a local get-together, and it's always packed. I remain on the board of FRESHFARM Markets, which is one of the local greenmarket organizers in the Chesapeake Bay Area. We have eleven markets in the D.C. area, with 150 local growers and producers. I'm pleased to say that the total farmer/producer growth in sales is up 3,068 percent since the original market began in 1997, and our farmers come from five states—Delaware, Maryland, Pennsylvania, Virginia, and West Virginia—around the Chesapeake Bay watershed. It's a wonderful way of communicating agriculture and fresh food to a community—attracting 380,000 diverse shoppers annually and donating fifty thousand pounds of food to local charities per year—as well as being a financially successful nonprofit. Even today, I almost never miss the Dupont Circle farmers' market on Sunday and am very proud to have been part of its creation.

Even with the development of the market ongoing, I was always on the lookout for new vendors for my restaurant. One rainy Saturday, while driving through the Cleveland Park neighborhood, I saw a truck parked with a sign that said, "New Morning Farm, Organic Produce." I stopped and went over to a man selling gorgeous produce from the truck. I asked if he was the farmer, and if he was organic, and he said yes to both.

"You're my man!" I told him, to his surprise. Jim Crawford lived in southwestern Pennsylvania, about two hours from

D.C. "I need more local organic produce," I said. "Would you grow for me and do business with my restaurant?"

He said yes but had even bigger plans. He told me he was in the process of putting together a co-op, the Tuscarora Organic Growers Cooperative. In his area, there were many Amish and Mennonite family farms that barely made a living. They were struggling to compete with large agribusiness at a complete disadvantage. Jim wanted to help them become certified organic and become co-op members. Together, they could hire a manager and truck drivers, get storage and refrigeration units, and sell to restaurants and other food establishments or markets in the volume necessary to survive.

I told him that would be great. It would be so much easier for me to deal with a co-op than lots of individual farmers. Over time, I let him know what I needed for my restaurant—celeriac, fingerling potatoes, arugula, rhubarb, berries, zucchini flowers, and all types of lettuces and squashes—and promised to buy them if he grew them.

Jim was trying to expand his co-op's clients, but few chefs knew about his work. I knew a lot of D.C. chefs, so I suggested that I call them all up, rent a small bus, and take them out to the farm. Public Voice for Food and Health Policy once again came through and helped out with the expenses.

We met on a Monday, when most restaurants are closed. About a dozen chefs gathered outside Restaurant Nora, and we drove out to Pennsylvania. It was fun; it felt like a field trip. We arrived at a Mennonite farm, which was small, perhaps ten acres, and had lots of different vegetables growing. It was beautiful; instead of huge crops, it looked like a big family garden. You wanted to walk around and pick a leaf here and a tomato there and taste everything. It smelled like fresh dirt and fragrant herbs and vegetables.

The Mennonite women, in their little white caps, had prepared a lunch for us on the second floor of a big old barn. For many of the young chefs, who rarely got out of the city, it was a real scene. They were astonished to find farms so close by; many of them had gone to culinary school but had never even been out to see where their food was being grown. The Mennonites had set up farm tables, and on each one sat a big basket of fried chicken, biscuits, and string beans. For dessert, we had shoofly pies and mud pies.

The Mennonites told us about their farms. The co-op had been great for them, especially for the Amish farmers who depend on their neighbors for motorized transport. This way, they could just deposit their vegetables in a shed on their land, and Jim would arrange to have them picked up and sold. Before the establishment of the co-op, the Mennonite farmers had mainly grown Early Girl tomatoes, yellow corn, and iceberg lettuce—nothing special. Jim introduced them to more varied and specialized crops that chefs were looking for, which could command higher prices.

Our day was a huge success. Some of the chefs, such as José Andrés—who would later win a James Beard award—still tell me they fondly remember eating lunch in that barn and being introduced to the farmers face-to-face. Andrés had been buying things from California and Europe and had no idea he could source ingredients so close to home. Given the response we got that day, I continued doing those tours for a few more years, and the Tuscarora co-op still invites all the chefs to a big supper once a year, prepared by the farmworkers, with vegetables straight from the farm. These days, the co-op does millions of dollars' worth of business. When we started, it was struggling. Because of the co-op, and the interest from the chefs, all these small Amish, Mennonite, and family farms have been able to survive—and thrive.

Concurrent with the growth of the original FRESHFARM Market in 1997 and my work with the Tuscarora co-op, I began working to make organic produce more widely available from another source: the grocery store. At this juncture, large food conglomerates were beginning to realize that there was an emerging market for organic and natural foods. A Maryland-based company called Fresh Fields opened several stores in the D.C. area, selling both organic and conventional produce, as well as natural supplements and vitamins. They contacted me to help them develop more prepared organic items for their deli cases.

What was great about Fresh Fields was that the stores not only sold organic produce but also educated people about why they should spend fifty cents more a pound for their organic peaches or strawberries. There was an information booth that explained everything that went into organic farming. The customers learned that organic produce was priced higher because organic farms tend to be smaller and have lower production, because they don't use pesticides, fungicides, or artificial fertilizer. Prices are also higher because there is more manual labor required and fewer machines; fields need to be weeded by hand rather than sprayed with pesticides, and compost needs to be prepared and tended, to fertilize the soil. And the farmers embrace a whole philosophy of organic farming, which is entirely different from big agribusiness. Instead of exploiting the land for all it can produce and leaving it devastated, organic farming recognizes that the earth sustains us and feeds us and that healthy soil must be maintained.

As Fresh Fields' new research and development chef, I introduced low-fat dips, such as hummus and guacamole, as well as veggie burgers, sesame spinach, spicy green beans—a lot of delicious foods customers could take home. I even created a complete organic dinner—seared salmon, sautéed greens or green beans, roasted potatoes or potato salad, for instance—but it was a little early for people to spend ten dollars for a dinner from the deli case. Now, of course, those kinds of prepared organic dinners are very popular.

Later, in 1996, when Whole Foods was interested in buying Fresh Fields, I began to worry that the focus would shift to the bottom line, including how much money my prepared foods were bringing in. Fresh Fields scratched me off the payroll before the deal went through, though Whole Foods continued to make some of my recipes but not with organic ingredients, which was a shame. Whole Foods understood that it had to expand nationally in order to be successful. It started buying up small natural and organic markets all over the country; Fresh Fields was one of them. It was a question of economies of scale, and it chose to have the ability to offer lower-priced products nationwide, but sacrifices were made in the process.

After Fresh Fields, I started working with Walnut Acres, the first organic mail-order business, which originated in the 1940s. I was hired to write a monthly newsletter for its catalog, to inspire subscribers to buy its organic products. I also developed packaged mixes, such as organic risotto mixes, soup mixes, and cookie dough mixes. It was an attempt to bring the convenience of a prepared mix with the benefits of organic food to a busy consumer. It was a great experience; I learned a lot about the wider organic industry, though it was not ultimately successful with regard to the products. A wonderful woman named Camilla Rothwell became my assistant and helped me enormously with these consulting jobs, testing recipes and writing newsletter copy. She had run a catering business in England and was extremely helpful to me. After 2011, Steven felt the restaurant couldn't afford to pay for an assistant for me, so he promoted her and made her director of special events, a position she still holds today. She is essential to our business.

It was while I was working with Walnut Acres that I went to the Natural Products Expo in Anaheim, California, in 1997. Bob Anderson, the owner of Walnut Acres and a passionate believer in the importance of organic food, took me to dinner. As we perused the menu, I asked the waiter where the different ingredients came from—where the fish was caught, who farmed the lettuce, whether the peaches were organic, and so forth.

"Wow," Bob said, "you're really serious."

He then asked me about how I acquired all the organic ingredients for my restaurants. It was incredibly satisfying to talk with someone who was as passionate about organics as I was and who respected the way I thought.

"Nora," Bob said, "it's unbelievable the lengths that you go to in order to find your organic ingredients. You have so much that's already organic on your menu. You go to all this trouble—why don't you see if you can have the restaurant certified organic, too?"

It took me a while to digest the idea. Bob was right: I was going to a great deal of effort to make everything organic, but it was still difficult to translate the importance of this message to my diners. Perhaps if I were certified organic—the first restaurant in the country to be designated as such—it would give me more credibility and help my customers understand why I was so passionate about the importance of organic food. To be certified organic by a third party would perhaps take the organic movement a step forward in the restaurant world.

But I had no idea what would be involved or if it were possible. "No one's ever done that before," I told Bob.

He waved away my concerns; he was very enthusiastic about the idea. "You just have to find a certifier who will do it for you."

I started asking around at the expo about certification agencies. The first people I tried all told me that certifying a restaurant couldn't be done. Others said it would be such an unbelievable hassle and expense that it wouldn't be worth it. Fortunately, I was introduced to Yvonne Frost, the president of Oregon Tilth, a certifying agency in Corvallis. She was very approachable, a maternal-looking woman in her fifties, with blond haired pulled back into a loose bun. When I asked her about the possibility of certifying my restaurant, she was intrigued.

"That's a really interesting idea," she said. "But we'd basically have to create the standards ourselves."

Yvonne was very encouraging from the start. She knew something about restaurants, too. In her younger, hippie days, she'd run a little grocery store and deli. She started thinking out loud. "A restaurant is many things," she said. "It's like a combination of a farm, a store, a commissary, and a distributor." Organic standards had already been created for those kinds of things, so it should be possible to cobble them together to create standards for a restaurant.

"Why don't we try it?" she said. "It'll take a while, since it's never been done before. But there's a first time for everything."

Yvonne said the first step would be to find a lawyer to research what it would take for a restaurant to become certified; one of her staff members was working toward her law degree, so she could take that on. There were a lot of rules. Ultimately, I would have to prove that at least 95 percent of everything that came into the restaurant came from organic sources.

I was thrilled. "Let's do it," I said.

Over the next two years, Yvonne mailed me lots of regulations, thick documents I had to go through. Some of the regulations made no sense for a restaurant, because they were intended for enormous commercial enterprises, like washing down the stainless steel walls every night. When the rules didn't apply, we made modifications.

All of my purveyors would have to be certified organic—not just the farmers, but every product that came into the restaurant, including oils, vinegars, spices, herbs, coffee, flour, and sugar. The certification applied only to food, but I took it a step further and made sure all my cleaning products were biodegradable and nontoxic. The 5 percent of my products that were allowed to be nonorganic had to be stored separately from everything else. We had to have an extensive paper trail, with the certificates of every purveyor filed each year.

It was an enormous challenge, but I enjoyed it. Many of the farmers I already used grew organic produce but had never been certified. Some of them felt certification was just bullshit paperwork: They'd been organic all this time, so why did they need to pay for certification to document something they were already doing on their own? It took me a long time to convince some of them, and in a few cases I had to find new farmers.

Other organic ingredients were really difficult to source. I found organic olive oil but packaged in such small, high-priced bottles that it would have raised my food costs exorbitantly. I had to find wholesalers and get it delivered in big drums. I found organic sugar, but it was only sold in quantities of a thousand pounds at a time, so we had nearly a whole room stacked with sugar. The only organic salt we could find we had to import from Sicily.

If you're organic, you depend on the seasons much more than conventional farmers, who can manipulate ripening using sprays and other techniques. It's possible, of course, to get organic fruits out of season, but it's usually from far away, like Chile or Mexico, which I try to avoid. I do buy things like avocados and oranges from California, but I try to limit my purchasing to North America. It just doesn't make sense to me to buy organic cherries from Israel. At my restaurant, I always adhered to the season. If it was the season for greens, we used them everywhere. In the fall, apples are all over the menu. Organic produce is often more expensive than conventional. A case of organic lemons, for instance, can be as high as 30 percent more expensive than conventional, and they're not always available. One of the reasons organic food costs more is because it isn't federally subsidized. There is less demand for the product and fewer farmers; more manual labor is required to maintain the fields, to compost, and to undertake natural pest control, which is often not as effective as chemical pesticides, in turn reducing the yield. So I limit the lemons I buy, which is difficult for bartenders, because everyone wants a lemon twist. I try to get them to offer a lime slice instead; limes are easier to grow, and there is a higher demand for them, so they are more plentiful. Those are the kinds of small concessions you have to constantly make to be fully organic.

We also had to make a lot of products ourselves. We produced our own ice cream because there was nothing organic out there at the time, and the same was true of our pasta. We of course made our own baked goods and cakes, using only organic sugar, eggs, butter, flour, nuts, and chocolate. We weren't able to get special chocolate for glazes or other uses; there was only one option. Steven, who is responsible for our wine program, focused on sourcing wine from small vineyards. He bought wines made mainly with organic grapes; he also noted on the list which wines are certified organic.

We had to do our own laundry because the laundry service used a ton of bleach and chemical cleaning products. I installed machines in the basement, where we use biodegradable soap. Our carpet is biodegradable, too—one of the biggest contributors to landfill is wall-to-wall carpet. I made sure all my pots and pans were stainless steel or cast iron, not aluminum. We used low-volatile-organic-compound paint; we installed a sophisticated water filtration system. But inevitably we had to make certain exceptions. I tried to have organic tablecloths, but the laundry service rebelled because the hemp-and-cotton blend was so difficult to iron. As for cleaning products, Yvonne suggested vinegar for everything. You can't, however, use just vinegar when you have people handling vegetables and meat; the risk of food contamination is too high. For safety reasons, we accepted the fact that we have to wash the cutting boards and knives every night with a bleach solution. Technically, the organic certificate pertains only to our food, but I have tried to expand as much as possible to include everything in the restaurant. In the end, very little in my restaurant is not organic, and of the 5 percent that is allowed to be nonorganic, some of the ingredients are wild. Strangely, anything grown wild, like mushrooms or wild-caught fish, cannot be certified as organic. To me, anything wild should be organic. But because you can't trace exactly where those foods come from, and you don't know if they've been raised in polluted waters or covered in acid rain, they can't be classified organic.

The process was so complicated it's no wonder I was the first restaurant to get certified! Running an organic restaurant is expensive. It helps that I am a war child: I do not like to waste a single scrap, so I function quite frugally. But it is also expensive not simply because of the certification fee but because you need so many more staff. I have a full-time buyer who does nothing but source new organic purveyors and handles the complicated ordering process. Because we buy from nearly thirty different farmers, the buyer also has to coordinate their different schedules and delivery dates. He's in charge of keeping a two-hundred- to three-hundred-page book up-to-date with every purveyor's organic certificate. Some farmers go out of business, and some don't keep up their certification. I also have a full-time butcher, and I have a person who cleans and preps the vegetables that come from the farmers. We also employ two people who do the laundry in-house, unlike other restaurants. A maintenance person takes care of our extensive water filtration system in addition to his normal fix-it duties. It is a full-time, full-service operation, with more than fifty employees.

Finally, the day came when Yvonne called to say she was coming to inspect the restaurant. She had a phobia of flying, so she took the train from Oregon all the way across the country. She spent an entire day going through the restaurant and all our books. Yvonne was impressed with all we had done to adhere to the standards. In 1999, she gave Nora's its first organic certification. Steven made a big banner to hang outside, proclaiming that we were the first certified organic restaurant in the United States. Both *The Washington Post* and *The Wall Street Journal* covered the story; the *Journal*'s headline read, "And the Organic Oscar Goes To . . ." I was very pleased to have this official certification finally complete. Years later, when I was given an award from the Organic Trade Association, I was deeply honored, and I knew it would never have happened without Yvonne's hard work.

My lifetime—and career—have paralleled the rapid changes in our food system over the past forty years. After we became certified organic at Restaurant Nora, it made me think about how far we'd come. Before World War II, there was no such thing as organic food. All food was organic. Food was just food— plants, grains, meats, and dairy that we could all recognize or grow. There were no long lists of ingredients on packages that you couldn't pronounce, much less have any idea what they did to your body or the environment. In 1938, the USDA's *Yearbook of Agriculture* was called *Soils and Men,* and it remains a handbook of organic farming today, but back then that was the norm.

In 1941, twenty million Americans planted Victory Gardens to support food production during World War II—the kind of garden Michelle Obama planted at the White House. People learned to grow food to help sustain their families and to dig root cellars to store vegetables and to make pickles and preserves. In 1942, Rodale published *Organic Farming and Gardening* magazine, and in 1943—the year I was born—Sir Albert Howard, a British mycologist and agricultural researcher, published a classic text on soil fertility and was the founder of the organic farming movement, farming that creates the healthiest and most nutritious and sustainable soils.

But World War II changed everything, including the foods we eat. All the chemicals developed during the war, and the industry that created them, had to be turned to some sort of domestic use, which became, in part, chemical fertilizers and later pesticides, fungicides, and herbicides. Subsequently, as big agriculture grew, the use of pesticides and herbicides swept the nation, and chemicals were used to preserve our foods, feed our farm animals, and pollute the entire ecosystem right down to our stomachs. Diverse varieties of vegetables disappeared as big food industries decided what would be the most convenient, and least perishable, to sell in supermarkets. In eighty years, we lost 90 percent of the variety of our food seeds. Housewives became convinced that processed foods were more convenient and tasty, and they were spoon-fed recipes that required canned and packaged foods. The food system degraded into the horror of a supermarket I encountered in Washington, D.C., when I first arrived from Europe and couldn't find anything that resembled real, fresh, unaltered food except some lifeless iceberg lettuce and tasteless tomatoes.

In 1962, Rachel Carson published *Silent Spring*, a landmark environmental book that documented the negative impact of agricultural chemicals, especially DDT. Her groundbreaking work inspired the environmental movement and a turn away from pesticides in our food. In 1970, Earth Day was established by Senator Gaylord Nelson, and twenty million Americans took to the streets to demonstrate their concern for a healthy environment.

In 1971, Alice Waters opened Chez Panisse. Rodale Press started an organic certification program in California, which grew in the 1970s to other states, creating standards for people to know where their food came from and if it was free from chemicals. The International Federation of Organic Agriculture Movements (IFOAM) was organized in 1972, which added political clout to organic farming, and California Certified Organic Farmers (CCOF) was created in 1973 to provide standards for organic food. The Oregon Tilth certification agency started in 1974. It was 1976 when I started the Tabard Inn.

From this vantage point, I can see now how, in the late 1970s, the movement grew, in local food stores, politics, and culture. When you were in the thick of it, it was hard to feel as if it were a movement, but today it's clear that's what was happening. In 1977, Wendell Berry, a hero of mine, wrote *The Unsettling of America: Culture & Agriculture*, which argued the importance of the spiritual dimension of good farming. He described how agribusiness is unhealthy not only for our bodies and the soil but for our souls. Without a connection to land and farming, we become estranged from land and nature and how to care for them; our alienation from farming and the land breaks down our sense of community, devalues human work, and ultimately destroys nature in the service of economics. Berry was way ahead of his time and provided a spiritual and philosophical framework for the young organic movement.

In 1978, Governor Jerry Brown of California signed the Direct Marketing Act, which made farmers' markets legal. (Imagine: it was illegal to sell produce directly to consumers before then!) This began to change the way people related to their food, and got to know where it came from, and provided a means of encouragement and support to small farmers. The Organic Food Act was signed into California law in 1979, the year I opened Restaurant Nora.

Earlier in this chapter, I talked about the significant events of the 1980s and the groundbreaking passage of the 1990 farm bill. Over the course of the ten years after the farm bill first laid the groundwork for organic standards, the U.S. government finally announced its new organic standards. The conventional food lobby is very strong, and so it had been a real struggle to put meaningful standards into play. Initially, the USDA had proposed allowing bioengineered crops, sewage sludge, and irradiation in organic production, which was hardly in keeping with the philosophy of tending the land to nurture its health. It is some measure of how popular the organic movement had become by then that the USDA was inundated with more than

300,000 consumers complaining about the regulations. In October 2002, when the final National Organic Standards were implemented, those "big three" exceptions had been removed. Finally, there was a nationally recognized set of standards so that consumers could understand what "organic" meant, and it spurred the growth of the market for organic produce.

We held a party at Restaurant Nora to celebrate, which Elizabeth Becker used as the backdrop in a story she wrote about organics in *The New York Times*. One of the people she quoted was David Cole, chairman of Sunnyside Farms and Acirca Inc., a company that acquires organic food companies. "This is the single biggest step in the last 100 years to change a broken agriculture system that puts profits above all else," he said. When the guidelines were implemented, the government, in conjunction with the organic industry, established the National Organic Standards Board, with members representing all agricultural sectors, so that these standards could not be adjusted or exploited.

As the owner of the first certified organic restaurant in the country, I was invited to speak at a press conference held by the Environmental Working Group in front of a room filled with politicians and environmental experts. I was intimidated speaking to a crowd, but I was thrilled that the standards had finally been established and the public could understand the vast difference between conventional and organic food. It was a huge validation of my efforts and of the organic foods movement as a whole.

It followed, then, that through the decade the importance of eating locally became much more widely understood. Authors such as Michael Pollan, with his 2006 *Omnivore's Dilemma: A Natural History of Four Meals,* and Barbara King-solver, with her 2007 *Animal, Vegetable, Miracle: A Year of Food Life,* promoted the notion that you should eat foods that are not grown too far away. Farmers' markets, once rare, became ubiquitous around the country; there are now more than eight thousand.

Organic foods became more widely available and more in demand. Sales of organic foods grew from twelve billion dollars in 2004 to thirty-two billion dollars in 2012. One of the great effects of this growth is that the price of organics is going down. It's always been a problem that organic food has been seen to be elite—much more expensive and mainly available to people with money. To have it more widely available to more people at a lower cost is a great step forward, and I'm all in favor of having organic foods available at large commercial stores like Walmart and Costco, because that's where people shop. It's great if you can shop for local produce at farmers' markets, but if you can't, the more organics that are available, the better. I still think, however, that if you can buy both—local and organic—this is the best option.

At the same time, we need to reconsider what we spend our money on. Most of the inexpensive food available in the United States is not of good quality. It is less healthy, it is not high in nutritional value, and it is grown for quantity, not quality. It is also high in animal fat and refined carbohydrates and low in fiber and has contributed to our obesity epidemic and other health problems. It's bad for our health and for the environment. Organic foods and produce benefit our health and help to preserve biodiversity. Paying more for these items supports farmers who keep our environment clean, protects the health of farmworkers, and helps to sustain rural communities. In the long run, "cheap" food has a staggering cost. I always say that I prefer to spend my money on food now rather than medical bills later.

Today, some 78 percent of families buy some organic foods now and then. But sales of organic foods and beverages still represent only 4.2 percent of all food sold in the United States. Less than 1 percent of all American crops are organic, so we have a long way to go. Someday, we can hope to be like Europe, where fully 25 percent of all agricultural land is certified organic. We are steadily moving in that direction, and the latest farm bill, from 2014, was a real win for the organic movement, in that it provides money for research and certification programs and to develop the science and technical assistance to transition farmers, support organic growers, and help grow the organic sector overall. This farm bill dramatically expands opportunities for organic farmers. The government is responding, at last, to consumer demands for food that is healthy and hazard-free.

Of course, every successful movement has a backlash, and the organic movement is no exception. In 2012, the media made one of their occasional nutritional pronouncements. "Organic Foods Not Healthier," read headlines around the world. A Stanford University meta-study on organic versus conventional produce was ripe for misinterpretation. It claimed that eating organic doesn't give you health benefits, but the scientists just measured nutrients in the foods without taking a look at pesticide residue or antibiotic resistance, both of which have been proven to be harmful to our health. Numerous studies are also coming out that show that pesticides have adverse effects on our hormones and may be contributing to obesity.

To me, "healthy" means that we aren't spraying toxic chemicals on the food we eat, we aren't dousing agricultural workers with those pesticides, and we aren't poisoning the earth and its vital microorganisms with chemicals. "Healthy" means that we are nourishing the soil with compost, we're keeping the water clean, we're preserving the earth for future generations, and we are treating nature and our bodies with respect, not reckless disregard. "Healthy" means foods that are picked ripe and bursting with flavor and nutritional value, that are so delicious that children and adults alike will want to eat their fruits and vegetables. And more fruits and vegetables, we do know, mean better health.

CHAPTER 10

Digestif

One winter day in 2010, I was standing in the kitchen of Restaurant Nora between two Secret Service agents. While the chefs and line cooks were busy slicing and sautéing, the agents grilled me with questions about the food and the staff, because First Lady Michelle Obama would be having her surprise birthday party upstairs.

When I first came to Washington, D.C., as a young housewife and began to teach low-budget gourmet cooking classes, I could never have imagined I might one day be in this position. So it was incredibly satisfying—after three decades of trying to get organic foods, and my certified organic restaurant, recognized—to have the first lady at Restaurant Nora for her birthday dinner.

I'd had other presidents and first ladies visit the restaurant, but I was especially happy to host Michelle Obama. She is such an amazing role model for children and young women in this country—so gracious, spirited, and talented. We share a lot of values about living a healthy lifestyle. I admire her program for kids, Let's Move, and her focus on preventing childhood obesity. She has made such a tangible difference in the health of the nation, including her initiative to promote exercise and healthy eating. She understands that you have to teach people to eat well and exercise from an early age, not only to prevent illness, but to help them be happy and motivated people who can contribute something to our society. And what an inspiration to everyone to put a garden at the White House!

So I was thrilled that she was coming to the restaurant. Valerie Jarrett called to say that it would be a surprise party. We'd gotten another phone call from her office, suggesting that our menu include lots of shellfish and mentioning that the first lady likes to eat simply prepared, flavorful food. I created a menu, which was approved by her staff, and then the Secret Service arrived the morning of the event to check out the upstairs room where the first lady would be dining. I asked if the president would be coming too, but they said no.

Before the meal, everyone in the restaurant was very excited, tiptoeing around as the agents peppered me with questions. Everyone had to go through a security check, and those who had access to our private dining room needed special badges giving them clearance. The agents positioned someone in the front of the restaurant so that all the regular diners would be checked upon entry as well.

I had made a simple four-course menu with several options

and served wine from Spottswoode, as well as from Domaine Pouillon, my son's winery in Washington State's Columbia River Gorge. I was in the kitchen, overseeing preparations, when I heard the Secret Service man next to me radio, "They're leaving now. They will be arriving here in seven minutes."

I turned to him and raised an eyebrow. "They?"

"I can't tell you," he said.

I began to get excited.

When I looked out the window, after what really was seven minutes sharp, police cars had blocked off the street, and a black limousine whizzed around the corner. The door opened, and out climbed the president and the first lady. They looked wonderful—so attractive and energetic, with brilliant smiles. They went straight to the back entrance to go upstairs. When they opened the door, Michelle really was surprised to see more than twenty people at her birthday party. She didn't expect it; she thought that she and her husband were just going out on a dinner date.

The first lady asked for a simple green salad to start, then the rack of lamb, and after that the molten chocolate cake with cappuccino ice cream, which I'm glad she enjoyed on her birthday. The president had soup, scallops, lobster—he was the person who wanted shellfish, it seems—and after, apple pie with whipped cream. After the food was served, I went upstairs. Valerie Jarrett introduced me to the president, explaining that I was the owner of what is the first certified organic restaurant in the country.

The president greeted me and called to Michelle from across the table.

"Michelle! Michelle!" he said. "You have to meet this woman! Nora's is the first certified organic restaurant in the country."

The first lady was very gracious and shook my hand. "It's wonderful what you are doing," she said. "I'm so happy to be here." When the first lady returned to her seat, the president studied me and said, "I've seen you before."

"Yes, we've met. I can't believe you remember!" I told him.

"At the White House garden," he said.

I truly couldn't believe he remembered meeting me. Sam Kass, personal chef to the Obamas and Senior Policy Advisor for Nutrition Policy, had arranged it, because I had some Finnish friends visiting; I had met them in Helsinki when I visited on a trip dedicated to establishing organic farmers' markets and inspiring organic farmers in Finland. We were just walking from the garden toward the White House, when the president came toward us with the president of Pakistan and his son and said, "Sam, who are these people?"

Sam said, "They're from Finland, and they wanted to see the White House garden. They're into food and farming." The president introduced us to the president of Pakistan and his son and said, "It's wonderful what you are doing, keep it up."

I said, "Mr. President, I'm Nora. I have the first certified organic restaurant in the country." And he looked at me and said, "That's wonderful! Next time I'm in Finland, I'll make sure to come and see you." Then he continued on his way. I had to laugh.

The Obamas had a good time at Michelle's party. They stayed nearly four hours, with a lot of Michelle's friends who came from Chicago for the evening. I asked the president if he would mind saying hi to everyone in the kitchen when they left, and he shook hands with the entire staff. I hadn't seen my employees so thrilled since Muhammad Ali came in, in the 1980s. When the Obamas walked outside, a big crowd had assembled, and everyone was shouting, "Happy birthday!" and cheering the couple on. It was a wonderful time.

It was an important evening, not only because the president and the first lady dined at Restaurant Nora, but because I never thought I'd see the day when I'd host a president and a first lady who were such proponents of a way of eating and living I've spent my life advocating. To have support for the cause in the Oval Office changes everything. I've spent most of my life in Washington, and I could never have dreamed that we'd have a president and, especially, a first lady who are so committed to promoting healthy foods. It made me realize how far we have come since the days when I felt as if buying organic meat were some kind of crime.

In 2014, we celebrated the thirty-fifth anniversary of Restaurant Nora. I'm still very involved in the restaurant and pleased that in my corner of Washington, D.C., I have made a difference in how people eat and how they think about the connection between what they eat, their health, and the environment. By starting a producer-only market, I have also helped to support the farmers who bring us our food and who are the stewards of the land for the next generations.

Over the past few years, I've tried to take the message and mission of my restaurant out into the world. I believe in being generous with my time, money, and influence, to do what I can on many different fronts in the environmental movement. My definition of "health" has expanded beyond food and organic agriculture to the health of the entire ecosystem. We have a much bigger job trying to preserve the earth, which has suffered from our heavy use of pesticides and chemicals, our overdevelopment and pollution.

So I've joined many organizations to get to work. I remain on the board of FRESHFARM Markets. I see how consumers are beginning to realize that while the produce at the markets may be expensive, it is the true cost of what it takes a U.S. farmer to produce food and stay alive. I also got involved with SeaWeb, an organization that campaigned to change people's fish-buying habits so that we chefs can help save overfished species and the ocean. By partnering with other organizations and creating a movement called Give Swordfish a Break, we helped repopulate the overfished swordfish. With the Caviar Emptor campaign, we helped keep sturgeon from going extinct in the Caspian Sea. With Take a Pass on Chilean Sea Bass, we tried to bring awareness to the overfishing of the Patagonian toothfish, otherwise known as Chilean sea bass, the enormous popularity of which has made this species almost extinct. I am now especially careful to only serve sustainable fish in my restaurant. My partners and I started a sustainable-fish business called Blue Circle, which is available at Whole Foods and other stores under the name Changing Seas.

These days, I am also on the board of the Environmental Film Festival, because I believe that film is such a great medium to relay a message; seeing a movie about an environmental problem is much more likely to change your behavior than reading a newspaper article. I'm on the board of Earth Day Network, which strives to bring awareness that we are stewards of this earth, which is very delicate and needs our utmost efforts at preservation. I'm on the board of directors of the Amazon Conservation Team (ACT) and through this work have come to realize how important it is to save the Amazon—this green mass that creates oxygen, the lungs of the earth, filled with beneficial plants and ancient knowledge. After I saw the work that ACT did trying to help the indigenous people and their shamans, I was moved to visit them. I spent two weeks in Suriname, in northern South America, in the Amazon rain forest. I was amazed by the wisdom of the shamans, who knew all the beneficial parts of each plant—the roots, leaves, flowers, branches, bark—each with a different purpose. They'd point out a plant that is poisonous but helpful for some ailments. They would explain that the plant has different effects, depending on the time of year. I've always been a great believer in the healing powers of the food we eat, and these shamans had a knowledge of our bodies' relationship to the plants and the natural environment that was deeper than I could ever have imagined. ACT helps the shamans pass their knowledge on to the younger generation by building schools and clinics and preserving their land from development, so I am glad to support it however I can.

Closer to home, I am a founding member of Wholesome Wave, an organization started by Michel Nischan, a wonderful chef and also a great organizer. It concentrates on bringing fresh food to underserved communities to create a more vibrant and equitable food system for everyone. There is a big need for this program; in so many urban areas, it is very difficult to find good produce, let alone organics. Wholesome Wave has developed different programs to serve these communities, like the Double Value Coupon Program, where people on food stamps (now called SNAP) can use them at farmers' markets and get double the value of a single food stamp dollar, and the Fruit and Vegetable Prescription Program, which was established to benefit overweight and obese individuals who are at risk of developing diet-related diseases. Here community health-care providers distribute fruit and vegetable "prescriptions" that recipients can redeem at participating farmers' markets for fresh, locally grown produce.

Because I've always liked to be active, I also work with a number of other organizations. Until recently, I sat on the board of Women Chefs & Restaurateurs, which gave me its first Genesis Award. I offer an organic internship to five recipients each year who are interested in knowing more about how organic food is grown and purchased. Scholarship recipients come on a Sunday, stay at my house, and cook at Nora's until Thursday, then work at an organic farm on Friday and Saturday. On Sunday, they return to the Dupont Circle farmers' market with the farmer and help sell whatever they have harvested. I'm also on the advisory board of Chefs Collaborative, which I helped found, and I'm on the advisory board for the Center for Mind-Body Medicine, which looks at the interaction of mind and body function. I'm also involved with Rachel's Network, named after Rachel Carson, a group of female philanthropists who give money to environmental causes.

So I keep myself busy! I hope that with my work in these organizations and the organic industry, I can continue to make a difference in advocating for a healthy lifestyle. I like to think I've influenced chefs; so many now are interested in local and organic foods and source their produce and meats on their menus from local farms. For me, it's very satisfying to see that my life's work has come to some sort of fruition. To that end, in September 2014, a new organization called Chef Action Network—established to educate chefs to become involved in food policy—honored me at its inaugural event. I was "roasted" by the many chefs I have inspired and worked with over the years.

It has always been a challenge for me to combine my work and advocacy with a satisfying personal life. It's difficult for any busy person to create a semblance of balance in his or her life and harder, I believe, for women. I've always felt that balance in your life is vital, not only in what you eat, but in how much you work and play and how much time you spend with your family.

Events in my personal life began to shift back in 1999, the year I got the organic certification. That same year, Pierre was diagnosed with bone marrow cancer. Pierre and I had always remained close—technically, we were still married—and I still cared for him, and we cared for our sons together. Pierre died that May, and then in June my mother died. Mutti was eighty-six, so it was not unexpected as it had been with Pierre. A month later, I flew to Paris to scatter Pierre's ashes at a cemetery. Alexis and Olivier were in Europe too, and we all did it together. They helped me say good-bye to my mother as well. It was a strange, sad time. Steven remained my partner, both at home and in the business. Many people asked us how we could live and work together, and I always said that it was the only way for us to work. You need a partner who understands your work, the hours and dedication you have to put into it, so he doesn't get resentful. Steven's and my business relationship—with our third partner, Steven's brother Thomas—always worked very well, with no one stepping on anyone else's toes and our skills functioning in a complementary manner.

But around the time we sold Asia Nora, Steven and I hit rock bottom in our personal lives. Steven was tired of our business always being tied to me, with my eponymous restaurant. He wanted to start a new business in organic aquaculture. As with our restaurants, Steven, Thomas, and I are partners in this endeavor, and the business has grown to be very successful. It did, however, take Steven away from running the restaurant. The girls were out of the house, and it turned out he had fallen in love with their piano teacher, a much younger woman, years before, and they had been having a long-term affair. When people say "it broke my heart," I now understand what they mean. It was brutally difficult to try to comprehend how someone who had lived with another person for thirty-three years, and helped create a successful business and healthy family, could deceive me and throw it all away. My family has always been so important to me, and the hardest thing was that he broke up our family unit.

It has been over five years since Steven and I split up, and as it turns out, despite how rough our break was at first, I have reached a point where I am now okay with it. I remain sad that our family is no longer together, but Steven and I stayed business partners at Restaurant Nora and Blue Circle. I have also remained close with Steven's family. In the beginning of our relationship, Steven's mother, Nellie, was not very excited about us. But she eventually changed her feelings toward me, especially after I got pregnant, and still to this day we are very friendly and supportive of one another. Nellie regularly thanks me, telling me how happy she is that I have involved so many of her children and grandchildren in the restaurant. To that end, over the last few years, eight Damatos have worked at the restaurant: Steven and Thomas's sister Marguerite and their brother John Paul, and six of their children: Nina, Pilar, Maya, Andre, Leah, and Ezra.

. . .

From the start, Thomas has been a wonderful partner. He and I still share responsibility for the daily operations of the restaurant, and additionally, he takes care of my personal accounting and finances. He is my rock—I am blessed to have someone whom I trust 100 percent in my business and my life.

I am a mature European woman; I've faced a lot of personal difficulties, and I've moved on. I have my mission, my passion, my friends, and my children, who are following in my footsteps in their own ways.

These days, I'm quite happy. I stayed in the house that I love, and I'm very close to my children and grandchildren. I think the best thing I ever did was to have kids. I've always been busy, but I've tried to do a good job as a mother, to set an example for how they should live their lives and find work that really satisfies them, something for which they have a passion. I've always wanted my children to find their own ways of being happy in their lives, with people who love them and work they enjoy and that fulfills them, and I'm pleased that they seem to be doing so. I was not a mother who was around all the time, chauffeuring them from one activity to another or always watching over them. There were times when I couldn't spend as much time with them as I wanted, and I know my children were jealous of my time and resentful of the business. It was particularly difficult when Pierre and I split up, and the boys had a hard time understanding and forgiving me for not being around as much as they wanted. But I made sure that when I was home, I listened to them, I loved them, and we spent a lot of happy times outdoors together.

I've never been the kind of mother who preaches to her kids; they learned from my example, and to my enormous pride they are also involved in work that sustains the environment. My oldest son, Alexis, has a successful sustainable winery, Domaine Pouillon, in Washington State's Columbia River Gorge. He has found a great partner, Juliet, who complements him both at work in the winery and in his personality. They have a small child, Jean Pierre, named after Alexis's uncle and his father, and a baby, Genevieve. Alexis is growing grapes organically, and he is now working to make his vineyard biodynamic. When I visit, I feel happy seeing him taking my work in his own direction; I can sit outside sipping some of the wine he named after his father—a full-bodied red blend—and feel grateful we had this son.

Olivier has lived in Bali for more than twenty years. He has two children, Natasya and Lucas, and is married to Ita, a wonderful Balinese woman who is very supportive and helps out with the business. Olivier studied environmental science and has a waste management and recycling business in Bali. Olivier's daughter, Natasya, now lives with me in Washington, D.C., and is enrolled in an environmental studies program in college. I'm enormously pleased that this interest has now been passed down to the next generation.

Unlike my sons, my daughter Nina didn't go in the direction of an environmental career until now. She had been living in New York and working in the art world, where she was in charge of special events at MoMA PS1. But I am thrilled she has recently returned to Washington, D.C., with her husband, Jordan Hepner, and has come to work with Steven at Blue Circle.

I think Steven's and my breakup has been hardest on Nadia; I know she misses us being a family. It took her a while to find her direction, but now she is using her considerable linguistic gifts to study different sign languages at Gallaudet University; she knows Braille, too, so she can be an interpreter for the deaf and the blind. She is phenomenally talented at learning languages; by the time she was a teen, she could speak nine of them. She's very happy, which makes me very happy too, because she had to overcome so many challenges as a little girl. Now, at twenty-five, she's coming into her own. She lives with Steven—and the piano teacher and her children—and the situation works well. Learning to communicate with her hands and touch, as Helen Keller did, is very fulfilling for her.

Being separated and single has been a big change for me. Having to deal with being alone, not having my children with me, and taking care of the business, the house, and the garden by myself have been challenging. But I'm fortunate that I often have a full house of visitors and guests, with whom I can cook and share meals.

Now, at seventy, I realize it is more important than ever to be careful and try to stay as healthy as possible, to live this last chapter of my life well. I take supplements, visit an acupuncturist and a chiropractor, and do a lot of exercise, whether it's dance, weight training, step classes, or going on walks with friends in Rock Creek Park once or twice a week. I love to ski and to spend time near the ocean. I like to keep my body in shape and my soul happy.

I look back on my life, and I can only say I'm proud of my children, my restaurant and its mission, the passion I have for my work, and my ability to influence many people in finding a happier, healthier lifestyle. I will continue in that direction as long as I can, hopefully inspiring people to work toward a more environmentally friendly future for humanity and the planet.

I still have dreams that organic food and a healthier lifestyle will become more accessible to everyone. Exercising and eating well are not just for the privileged. The poor eating habits and obesity that plague Americans are a cause of a slew of illnesses, such as hypertension, diabetes, cancer, and cardiovascular problems. It's crucial that we make it easier and more affordable for people to exercise and to eat more healthfully. I hope that will come to pass and that I will have played a small part in a more sustainable lifestyle for everyone. We may not see huge changes in my lifetime. But when I think back to my arrival in the United States in the 1960s and consider all the choices consumers have today, I can say that there has truly been a revolutionary change in the world of organic food. That gives me hope for a better future for us all.

Acknowledgments

I want to thank, of course, my agent, Deborah Grosvenor, who believed my story was worth telling, and who supported me throughout the entire process.

Thank you to Laura Fraser for helping me put my words on paper.

A big thank-you to my editor, Lexy Bloom, and her team at Knopf. Lexy loved my story and was crucial in making this book a reality. She went above and beyond her duties as editor, dedicating herself to *My Organic Life* and putting in the extra hours to make this book great.

I want to thank all of the organic farmers and distributors I have met over the years, who have supplied me with their products.

I want especially to thank Yvonne Frost of Oregon Tilth, who helped me make Nora's the first certified organic restaurant in the country. A big thank-you to Ann Yonkers for making the FRESH-FARM markets such a success, and for being a true supporter of my mission.

Restaurant Nora would not have flourished for all these years without my dedicated, loyal kitchen and dining room team—especially Camilla, Jack, Chi, Oanh, Efrain, Carlos, Marija, and German.

A special thanks to my first chefs, Alison Zaremba and Geoffrey Elliott, and to chefs Duncan Boyle, Jeff Olsson, Christian Thornton, Yuriko Matsuura, John Paul Damato, Haidar Karoum, Mark Hellyar, Benjamin Lambert, and Todd Woods.

And of course I want to give a thank you to all of my friends who have supported me. And a big hug especially to my business partners, Steven and Thomas Damato, for making my dreams and passion a reality.

A NOTE ABOUT THE AUTHOR

Nora Pouillon was born in Vienna in 1943. She moved to the
United States in the late 1960s and in 1979 opened Restaurant
Nora, which in 1999 became the first certified organic restaurant
in the country.

A NOTE ON THE TYPE

This book was set in Minion, a typeface produced by the Adobe
Corporation specifically for the Macintosh personal computer,
and released in 1990. Designed by Robert Slimbach, Minion
combines the classic characteristics of old style faces with the
full complement of weights required for modern typesetting.

Composed by North Market Street Graphics,
Lancaster, Pennsylvania

Printed and bound by Berryville Graphics,
Berryville, Virginia

Designed by Soonyoung Kwon